TURNING POINT

Christian America at the Crossroads

Compiled by ROGER ELWOOD

STANDARD PUBLISHING
Cincinnati, Ohio

5001

A word of special thanks is given to the seventeen authors who have contributed to this book. Standard Publishing is pleased to print their frank opinions, with the understanding that these do not necessarily reflect the policies or philosophy of the Company.

Library of Congress Cataloging in Publication Data

Turning point

   1. United States—Civilization—1970-　—Addresses, essays, lectures. 2. Education—United States—Addresses, essays, lectures. 3. Family—United States—Addresses, essays, lectures. 4. United States—Moral conditions—Addresses, essays, lectures.

E169.12.T87	973.92	80-17790

ISBN 0-87239-416-6

Introduction

A turning point is a historic period of time during which the course of the future of the human race is determined for better or worse. The Renaissance, the Reformation, and the Industrial Revolution all were turning points for man.

It is quite possible that we stand at such a juncture today. Tumult is a consistent barometer by which turning points can be ascertained. And what are we seeing about us right now? Enormous upheaval in terms of morals, economics, politics, religion; and on and on the list expands. Would anyone have dared to surmise, a couple of decades ago, that San Francisco would become a center of homosexual and other decadent activity? Or that abortion would be routinely performed in virtually every city in this nation? Or that pornographic bookstores and massage parlors would proliferate to the extent they have? Or that television would feed such blatant immorality into millions of homes, as now is the case?

In Romans 1 we read of an age in which "God gave them over to a reprobate mind." Are we at that kind of turning point today? Is more and deeper decline the end result? Or is this the "blow off," with more traditional values coming back in full measure just around time's corner?

There are four areas of concern in *Turning Point: Christian America at the Crossroads:*

The family.
The nation.
The school.
The church.

All four are in a state of turmoil. All four are so interrelated that eliminating just one would have resulted in a grossly incomplete picture. All four are of intimate concern to every Christian.

Some prominent authors have tackled subsidiary topics under each heading. Senator Jesse Helms, Dr. Clyde Narramore, Ben Armstrong, Dr. Paul Kienel, Dr. Harold Lindsell, and many more have lent their time and insights to the crucial issues being dealt with in the following pages.

To be uninformed is to be handing ourselves to the Great Deceiver as his hapless victims. Knowledge can be a very effective weapon for a Christian against the designs of Satan. Without that knowledge, particularly in the areas where he is most active, our hands are tied. We are as sheep before an impending slaughter.

But it is worse for us to *know*, to have our eyes opened about so much that is wrong in our world, and yet let apathy rule us. To be Christian is not enough; to be Christian and merely to realize that perversity exists is hardly the answer. Satan needs only the inactivity of all of us for his own master plan to hold greater sway.

—Roger Elwood
Agoura, California

Contents

Contributors

Carl A. Anderson is legislative assistant to Senator Jesse Helms; President of the American Family Institute; and an attorney admitted to practice in the State of Washington, the District of Columbia, and before the United States Supreme Court.

Ben Armstrong is director of National Religious Broadcasters. His recent book, *The Electric Church*, is considered a definitive treatment of the growing phenomenon of Christian worship via television.

Paul Copperman is a leading educator with principally secular schools and institutions. The author of *The Literacy Hoax*, he is considered one of the most conservative educators in the country, and is a leading foe of the National Education Association.

George Gallup, Jr., is presently heading The Gallup Organization, founded by his father, considered the top polling/survey company in the nation. A much-in-demand speaker across the country, he is becoming more and more involved in Christian subjects and activities.

Senator Jesse Helms represents the people of North Carolina in the U.S. Senate. A Republican conservative, he is one of the most respected members of the Senate, and a consistent opponent of ERA, abortion, and other liberal stands.

Dr. Gary Inrig is a Canadian pastor. He is a frequent contributor to leading Christian magazines and an author for Moody Press and other publishers.

Senator Roger Jepsen hails from Iowa. A Republican conservative, he is in his first year holding office as a U.S. Senator. He has worked at many levels of state government in Iowa, including the office of Lieutenant Governor.

Dr. Paul Kienel is director of the Association of Christian Schools International, the largest of the Christian private school groups in the country, with a quarter of a million students belonging to it. He is also a prominent author and a leader in quality education.

Dr. C. Everett Koop is co-author of *Whatever Happened to the Human Race?* (with Francis Schaeffer), which has been made into a multi-part film series. His previous publishing credits include *The Right to Live, The Right to Die,* a book dealing with abortion and other subjects. He serves as pediatric surgeon at Children's Hospital in Philadelphia, Pennsylvania.

Dr. E. LeRoy Lawson is minister of Central Christian Church in Mesa, Arizona. Among his publishing credits are *The Lord of Possibilities,* a study of the miracles of Jesus, and *Up From Chaos,* a study in the book of Genesis.

Dr. Harold Lindsell, former editor-in-chief of *Christianity Today,* is a much-in-demand lecturer. He has also written more than a dozen books, including *The Battle for the Bible,* which gives his views on Biblical inerrancy.

Jeanette Lockerbie is editor of *Psychology for Living,* a monthly publication sponsored by the Narramore Christian Foundation, Rosemead, California. She has co-authored *Surgeon of Hope,* the autobiography of Dr. Ralph Byron, prominent surgeon at the City of Hope Hospital.

Dr. John MacArthur is pastor of Grace Community Church, Sun

Valley, California. He has written several books, including *The Charismatics*, and some very fine commentaries. His daily radio program is heard throughout the country.

Dr. Clyde Narramore is the internationally-known psychologist and family counselor who founded the Narramore Christian Foundation twenty years ago. The foundation is now the largest of its type in the country.

Professor *Neil Postman* has been involved with the New York University School of Education for more than 20 years. He is a highly respected author in the secular community; his most recent book is entitled *Teaching as a Conserving Activity* (Delacorte).

Phyllis Schlafly, a Constitutional lawyer, is acknowledged as the most outspoken opponent of the Equal Rights Amendment. Her books include *The Power of the Positive Woman*, and she has published a monthly *Phyllis Schlafly Newsletter*. She is head of Eagle Forum, a coalition of men and women across the country who are attempting to stop ERA and the spread of abortion.

Knofel Staton teaches New Testament at Ozark Bible College in Joplin, Missouri. His many books include *Check Your Lifestyle*, a study in the book of Proverbs, and *How to Understand the Bible*.

PART ONE

THE SCHOOL

The Literacy Hoax

by Paul Copperman

Between 1900 and the mid-1950's, the academic achievement of America's students registered gradual improvement. This trend accelerated between 1957 and the mid-1960's as a result of the increased curricular rigor induced by *Sputnik*. In the mid-1960's heightened public concern about education broke the logjam preventing federal aid to education. For this and other reasons, our national education budget more than tripled between 1964 and 1976. This same period saw a sharp rise in the reading-readiness skills of our preschool children.

Yet the American educational system, flush with money and resources, enrolling children much better prepared than ever before in history, did not successfully teach these children their basic academic skills. Since the mid-1960's, academic performance and standards have shown a sharp and widespread decline. Today's eighth grader reads approximately as well as the average seventh grader just ten years ago and computes about as well as the average sixth grader of that period. On college admissions tests, only about a quarter of our current high-school graduates attain the level recorded by the average high-school graduate in the early 1960's. The decline in academic achievement has been measured in locales as disparate as Iowa and Hawaii, California and New York, Minnesota and Idaho. The decline is as evident in middle-class and upper-middle-class students as it is in disadvantaged students, as pronounced in students with above-average or even superior intelligence as in students of average or below-average ability. The academic skills of America's young people in the late 1970's have deteriorated to the pre-*Sputnik* level of the early 1950's.

The decline in educational standards is as sharp as the decline in basic academic skills. The amount and quality of academic work demanded of public-school students has been cut sharply. For one thing, students are simply not taking as many academic courses as they did in the early 1960's. As a percentage of high-school enrollment, enrollments in English, history, science, and math are sharply lower. Even the enrollment figures underestimate the reduction in the academic course load of the average student. Many traditional and rigorous courses have been replaced with fare best described as educational entertainment. Courses in film literature and science fiction are replacing English composition; courses in contemporary world issues and comparative revolutions are replacing world history. In these courses the amount of work assigned and the standard to which it is held are considerably lower than in the courses they replace.

Even in the more traditional classes, work demands and imposed standards have dropped considerably. The consensus is that the average student is assigned 50 percent less reading and writing than in the early 1960's, and that standards for written work are correspondingly low. High-school textbooks in most subject areas have been rewritten with a sharply reduced reading level, usually one or more years lower than the grade for which they are intended.

With skills down, assignments down, standards down, and grades up, the American educational system perpetrates a hoax on its students and on their parents. I have taken the liberty of applying a name to this successful piece of deception: I call it the literacy hoax.

America's public schools and colleges enroll over fifty million students each year. The overwhelming majority of them are repeatedly informed that they are acquiring an adequate or even excellent education. These students believe their report cards, their grade slips, and their teachers, counselors, and professors when these agents of the educational system tell them they have adequate academic skills, and are doing adequate or excellent schoolwork. In fact, many of these students suffer from a delusion of adequacy, engendered by an educational system which is lying to them.

In June of 1972 a young white male who calls himself Peter Doe graduated from a public high school in San Francisco. His school records show that he has an average IQ, and that during his twelve years of public schooling he achieved average grades, never had any discipline problems, attended school regularly, and was promoted every year. His parents testify that they frequently complained to school officials that he did not seem to have adequate reading skills. They were repeatedly assured that he was reading at the average level and had no special or unusual problems.

The first job Peter obtained after graduation was selling shoes. He lasted less than a week in this job because his reading skills were so poor that he could not do the minimal amount of paper work the job required. His reading skills were subsequently tested, and it was discovered that he was reading at a fifth-grade level. Peter sued the San Francisco United School District for a million dollars, arguing that he should not have been passed along from grade to grade without being taught the skills he needed at each grade level, and further arguing that by repeatedly lying to his parents, school officials had effectively prevented them from helping him obtain the remedial assistance he needed. When the California Supreme Court refused to hear an appeal of two lower-court decisions dismissing the suit, public-school educators across the land breathed a collective sigh of relief, because from 10 to 15 percent of our recent high-school graduates read no better than Peter Doe.

What can a functionally illiterate young adult do in modern American society? Join the welfare ranks, try burglary or prostitution or perhaps armed robbery—or go to junior college? A recent report indicates that over 50 percent of the entering students at San Francisco's public two-year college read at a fifth-grade level or below. Even the military has a hard time with these young people. A study recently reported by UPI indicates that over a third of the nation's naval recruits read below a tenth-grade level, and that 70 percent of these read so poorly they cannot complete their basic training. The UPI story tells of a sailor who did $250,000 damage to a ship's engines because he could not read a repair manual. As a result of this incident and other similar ones, the Chief of Naval Personnel has mandated a sixth-grade reading level as the minimum acceptable level for naval personnel, a standard which, of course, leaves out Peter Doe and over half the entering freshman class at San Francisco City College.

When one examines such a widespread phenomenon as the literacy decline of the past ten years, it is easy to become preoccupied with statistics and other abstract measures of performance. We forget that these statistics measure the ability of vulnerable human beings to survive and function in the world. Imagine how devastating it must be at eighteen years of age to discover that you are illiterate and incapable of holding a job.

There is a body of research which supports my belief that it requires a degree of competence in the primary academic skills to function in our society. A recent study indicates that it takes approximately a seventh-grade reading level to hold a job as a cook, an eighth-grade level to hold a job as a mechanic, and a ninth or tenth-grade level to hold a job as a supply clerk. I believe it is a reasonable inference that a job as a teacher, nurse, accountant, or engineer would demand a higher minimum level of reading ability. Many studies have found high correlations between reading disability and criminal behavior or juvenile delinquency, including a recent study which indicates that as many as 85 percent of the youngsters who appear in juvenile court are disabled readers. The recently conducted Adult Performance Level (APL) study shows that 40 percent of the adult population with incomes under $5,000 per year are functionally illiterate, compared to 8 percent of the population with incomes over $15,000 per year. When I judge course work or curriculum, my first question is, "Will this program promote the acquisition and development of the basic skills?"

I believe the second function of our educational system is to promote the development of what I call higher literacy. I define higher literacy as the ability to apply primary academic skills to the cultural and intellectual record of the society: history, literature, science, and mathematics. Education to higher literacy helps an individual make sense out of the world in which he lives by training his intellect to understand the bonds connecting places, times, and events. By teaching him to recognize the consequences of past actions, this type of education refines his decision-making ability and enables him more fully to realize his human potential. It allows him to participate actively in modern society, to feel that he is a part of the day-to-day events which shape his environment, and his life.

We live in a democratic society, one of the few free societies existing today; indeed one of the few that has existed since the dawn of civilization. We jeopardize our freedom if we do not make every attempt to teach all of our citizens the knowledge they need to make the good choices that will keep our democracy operating. The decline of academic achievement, the perpetration of the literacy hoax—these are harbingers of Huxley's brave new world and Orwell's world of 1984. Thomas Jefferson said it first and said it best: "If a nation expects to be ignorant and free, in a state of civilization, it expects what never was and never will be." In judging course work and curriculum, my second question is, "Does this program promote higher literacy?"

Between illiteracy and functional literacy, between functional literacy and higher literacy, is a continuum of skill and knowledge. I believe the key to movement along this continuum is the acquisition and refinement of the primary academic skills: reading, writing, and computing. The past ten years have witnessed a sharp decline in the acquisition of these skills by America's young people, a decline tragic in its consequences for the individuals it affects, and for our society.

The Media's Impact

by Neil Postman

During most of the 1960's and early 1970's, the word that received the heaviest pounding in discourses on education was "relevance." Every education writer, it seemed, was expected to work it over thoroughly, and I joined in the fun myself in at least two books I wrote.

The prevailing opinion in those years was that educational relevance meant that which was of immediate interest, controversial, and, if possible, entertaining. It followed from this that any relevant topic would engage the student's wholehearted attention, and by that sole virtue was deserving of inclusion in the school curriculum. The opposite was also held to be true: that which did not have an immediate and engrossing interest to a student was mere pedantry and a waste of valuable time.

By this definition of relevance, the best thing the schools could do would be to close their doors and turn the education of our youth over to the electronic media: television, film, records, and radio. For there can be no doubt that the media have our students' wholehearted attention, and that the "curriculum" of the media—*Star Wars*, Fonzie, The Who, and the like—has a direct and urgent bearing on our students' lives.

As a matter of fact, something very close to this has already happened. The average American child, from age six to 18, spends about 16,000 hours in front of a television set. The only activity that occupies more of an American youth's time is sleeping. And if we add to TV viewing time the amount of time spent listening to records and radio and watching movies, we get a figure in excess of 20,000 hours of "relevance."

Given the fact that the media are already the dominating force in the education of our youth, it is reasonable to ask if there is not some other definition of relevance that might be used by the schools during the 12,000 hours our students are required to be there.

I believe there is, and it may be simply stated: What has the most relevance to students is that which their culture least provides them. This is what Cicero meant when he said that the purpose of education is to free a student from the tyranny of the present. It is also what Andre Gide meant in saying the best education is that which goes counter to one's culture.

I call this the thermostatic view of schools. It may also be called the ecological view, which is to say that schools should try to keep the education of our youth in balance. When the culture stresses yin, the schools should stress yang. In this way, there is a continuous dialogue sustained between competing points of view: the teachings of the culture and the teachings of the school. Through this dialogue, students are protected against being overwhelmed by the biases of their own times—for to leave students entirely to the influences of the dominating biases of their culture is to guarantee them a one-dimensional education and a half-developed personality. What is relevant, therefore, is what the culture is insisting is irrelevant.

In our present circumstances, we may look directly at the electronic media to discover what are the dominant teachings of the culture. The media teach many things, of course, but I should like to mention four of their biases which are in special need of opposition by schools.

The media are, first of all, attention-centered. Their main goal is to capture and hold the attention of their audiences. The content of media is of relatively little importance. It is changeable and disposable. Its only function is as bait.

Second, the media are vastly entertaining. Nothing will appear on TV or the movie screen outside of school unless it has "entertaining value." This means it must not be demanding or disturbing, for if it is, the audience will turn away.

Third, the media, especially television, are image-centered. TV consists of fast-moving, continuously-changing visual images which compress time to an extraordinary degree. The average length of a shot on "The Love Boat," for example, is about three seconds. On commercials, the average length of a shot is two seconds. (In the first 20 years of their lives, American children will see approximately 500,000 TV commercials.) Thus TV, as well as movies, work against the development of language.

Ironically, the two electronic media best suited to the transmission of human speech—the radio and phonograph—have been given over almost entirely to the transmission of music, a nonlinguistic form of communication. Such language as is heard on records is little else but comedy routines, or song lyrics at the level of Neanderthal chanting. On radio, language is largely a commercial message, mostly a parody of speech—disjointed, semihysterical, almost completely devoid of ideational content.

And finally, most of what children see on TV and in the movies takes the form of stories. The media ("Sesame Street" is no exception here) have turned all cultural teaching into a narrative mode. Exposition—the systematic presentation and development of ideas—is practically unknown among our children.

The teachings of the media, then, stress instant, not deferred, gratification; entertainment, not serious content; images, not words and stories, not ideas. According to the thermostatic view, our schools must now make a concerted effort to counterbalance such teachings. This would imply that the schools stress, for example, subjects that require students to understand and express themselves in words; that require them to pay attention even when they are not being entertained; that require them to evaluate and criticize ideas; that demand concentration and a confrontation with complexity. If you are under the impression that most of our schools already do this, you might find it sobering to know that more than half the high schools in the United States do not offer a single course in physics.

But I do not intend here to criticize what educators have been doing, and certainly do not want to associate myself with a simplistic "back to the basics" movement. The point I am making is that we can no longer ignore the extent to which the teachings of the media are controlling the direction of the intellectual character of our youth. In the future, the schools must promote, as never before, the skills, values, and behaviors that the media either disregard or undermine.

To be specific, I believe the schools must emphasize more than ever such subjects as history, science, and semantics. Even philosophy and comparative religion would be extremely valuable, especially for high-school students. Subjects such as these require students to confront serious content, complexity, and continuity. They are also uniquely able to provide perspectives on the present.

The processes of reading, writing, speaking, and listening should, of course, be given the highest priority. And it would be desirable if, at long last, our schools took seriously the teaching of critical thinking. But beyond the subjects we teach, the school may act as a thermostatic agent through its style and ambience. I believe it is important, for example, that school be sharply differentiated from other cultural institutions such as movie theaters, rock concert sites, and playgrounds.

It is particularly important that schools be seen as places of serious and dignified academic purpose. This implies that schools would attempt to preserve civilized modes of discourse and relatively formal patterns of behavior; that schools insist on a measure of respect for traditional social symbols; and that the schools undertake the task of teaching our youth how civilized intellects disagree with one another and generally what the habits are of well-mannered people.

In this way, we will be providing our youth with an alternative idea of relevance—an idea they may use to judge for themselves, in a changing future, what knowledge and values will serve most surely to conserve and enrich their own lives and the life of their culture.

Christian Schools:
Their Growing Impact

by Dr. Paul A. Kienel

Mr. Gable, tapping a small bell on his desk, said, "Class, please come to order. We will now salute the American flag." With hands over hearts, my four classmates and I stood proudly. We said solemnly, "I pledge allegiance to the flag of the United States of America . . ." The words were a bit awkward because it was my first day of school in the first grade. In fact, there were only five students in the whole school. There were twin girls in grade three, a girl in grade four and a boy in the eighth grade who had remained in that grade for several years. Lest you feel sorry for us in our little red schoolhouse nestled in the wheat fields of north central Oregon, please don't. It was an academic heaven! In the nineteen years of my formal education that followed, the quality of instruction never surpassed the learning intensity of that little public school in Oregon. I truly had five teachers, Mr. Gable and the four other students. They all helped me.

Our school's heating system consisted of a potbellied stove fueled by wood that we carried in. The restroom facilities were small one-room structures located on either side of the main schoolhouse.

Our school was deprived of an asphalt parking lot, landscaping, air conditioning, a multimedia learning center and even electricity. We didn't have any busing problems because there were no buses.

Our rural area was peopled by farmers who knew each other by name. They helped one another during harvest season and through difficult times. Our teacher, Mr. Gable, and other professional people, such as doctors and ministers, were highly revered in our community.

I consider myself fortunate to have begun my educational career at the end of a unique era. It was the trauma and heartbreak of war in the forties that shattered the tranquility of my early educational years. As our country mobilized for global war, Americans by the multiplied thousands moved from farming areas to the cities to work for the war effort. Sons and young fathers were drafted for military service. Family groups were separated and marriage bonds were weakened and often severed. Life for children during these years was unsettling. Even in rural Oregon we observed curfews and blackouts. We heard and saw the ominous aerial night practice missions over our community and along the cliffs and valleys of the beautiful Columbia River Gorge. Long caravans of U.S Army jeeps and trucks rumbled along our highways, especially at night.

The lifestyle of Americans changed rapidly during these years. Writing of the war years in his book, *The Family First*, Dr. Kenneth Gangel says:

> World War II defense plants reached their long, noisy arms into the kitchens of American families to create "Rosie the Riveter." While G.I. Joe was off shooting the bullets, his wife, girl friend or sister was back home making them. What apparently was not foreseen in those early forties was that the new working status of women was destined not to be a temporary stopgap measure to assist America in the war, but a whole new pattern of life which has now come to ugly fruition in what is loosely called the "Women's Liberation Movement." A cigarette commercial reminds American women, "You've come a long way, baby," but it stops short of suggesting which direction.

From the forties on, the climate of the classroom and the environment of the home would never be the same. The Bible-believing church community was a minor influence in the early forties. The tragedy of the Second World War came to a close in 1945, and Americans who had drifted spiritually saw their need for a basic Bible message. Old line liberal churches waned but Bible-preaching churches soared into prominence and popularity.

In the meantime, a counterforce was at work in the nation's

public schools. Secular public schools, based on a sterile secular philosophy, had no way of responding to a spiritual revival. They were responding to the philosophy of a man who believed that "traditional belief in God is an unproven and outmoded faith." He was the first president of the American Humanist Association. His name was John Dewey, Professor of Philosophy and Pedagogy at the University of Chicago and later at Columbia University. His views on pragmatic progressive education became the philosophic touchstone for all teacher-training institutions across America. His humanistic theories reached full force in the nation's public school system in the forties and continued into the seventies. Even though the public school system through the years has been peopled by more Christians per capita than any other profession in America, the ability of Christians to use the system as a means of presenting Christ was and still is severely limited. While the church was being revived in the fifties, sixties and seventies, the American home and our children's educational system lagged far behind.

It was my privilege recently to be an interview guest of Jess Marlow on the prime time *Channel Four Evening News* telecast, on the NBC affiliate in Los Angeles. Madaline Murray O'Hair had appeared on the same guest spot a few nights earlier. Along with the church and the family, she had also attacked Christian schools. I was asked to respond to her charges. As the interview began, I pointed out that "Madaline Murray O'Hair makes her living as a professional atheist, and in order for her to stay in the news, she has to make startling statements that keep her in the public's eye."

I was pleased in the course of the interview when the questioning turned from negative questions about Mrs. O'Hair to a positive line of questions about Christian schools. Jess Marlow was particularly startled that Christian schools are being established at the rate of three new schools a day across the U.S. The Christian school movement is the fastest growing educational movement in America.

The average American is not aware of the academic challenge of the future. The next generation is facing an information explosion. Dr. John MacArthur reports that the people of the world are currently producing 3,000 new pages of information every second and 60 million pages a year of new scientific and technical literature. Out of necessity, we are reducing this proliferation of information to ever smaller spaces for storage. Entire books can now be reduced to a one inch square piece of microfilm. Scientists have now developed laser storage, which can reduce the entire Library of Congress in Washington, D.C. to a space the size of a sugar cube!

The prophet Daniel predicted that in the end times, "Knowledge would increase" (Daniel 12:4). The following comparative figures will help you comprehend the incredible increase in knowledge in recent years. If all of man's knowledge from the beginning of history to 1845 is equal to one inch, then from 1845 to 1945 would equal three inches, and from 1945 to the present would equal the height of the Washington Monument or 622 feet.

It is obvious that youngsters in our schools now will need more academic skills than their parents. If our children are not academically equipped to master the scientific and moral challenges of the future, they will be subservient to those who can. Sadly, in the face of the information explosion and rapid increase in knowledge, academic skills in our public schools are gliding downward. Note these statistics:

1. Scholastic Aptitude Test (SAT) scores dropped again in 1979 for the 20th consecutive year, despite predictions that 1979 would show an upturn.
2. The National Assessment of Educational Progress found that only 42% of 17-year-olds tested could figure the area of a square when given the length of one side.
3. A Ford Foundation study says federal programs aimed at wiping out illiteracy have failed. As many as 64 million Americans may lack the reading and writing abilities needed for today's technologies.

It should not be too surprising then that the largest professional group among the parents who send their children to Christian schools are public school teachers and principals.

The following report comes from the "Educator's Newsletter" produced by the Northern Illinois Gas Company:

A rising number of middle-class families are reluctantly deserting public schools because they are unhappy with the quality of the education.

Many parents, putting a higher premium on fundamentals, want more challenging curriculum offered by many private schools. They also like the small classes, heavy homework loads and the easy access to teachers.

Since 1970, as the total number of U.S. school-age children declined, public school enrollment in nonsectarian public schools had advanced 60% to 1.8 million.

Teaching is also a hazardous job these days. It seems combat pay should come with regular salaries. More than 110,000 teachers in the U.S. public schools were attacked physically in their classroom during the 1978-79 school year.

Academic instruction in the government's public schools is hampered, not only by physical danger to teachers and students, but by the high cost of vandalism. The introductory paragraph of a recent government study of school vandalism states:

> School violence and vandalism are problems of increasing magnitude. Nationwide, over 5,000 teacher assaults are reported each month (National Safe School Study, 1978), and over $5,000,000,000 is spent each year to repair damage done by school-age vandals (Deegan, 1976). The Office of the Los Angeles County Superintendent of Schools (1979) reported that in school districts throughout Los Angeles County, the average vandalism costs were in excess of $5.5 million for only September through March in the 1978-79 school year, a 47% increase over the same period for 1977-78. . . . *Unfortunately, more is being spent on vandalism than on textbooks.*

In contrast, vandalism by Christian school students in Christian schools is barely measurable. Insurance rates for Christian schools are considerably less than they are for public schools. To my knowledge, not one Christian school uses a security guard to patrol the hallways and restrooms. Christian school students are not perfect and they sin and get rowdy like any group of immature mortals, but reasonable rules are established and violation of those rules results in appropriate consequences.

In California, the state and federal government allocated nearly $3,000 per child to operate its public schools in 1980. At $3,000 per youngster per year for twelve years, the total cost to taxpayers is $36,000, not including future inflation costs. Even the high cost of public education would be semi-tolerable, though, if the quality of instruction were higher. A witness testifying before the U.S. Senate Subcommittee on Education this past year said, "For the first time in the history of our country, the educational skills of one generation will not even approach those of their parents."

Paul Copperman's new book, *The Literacy Hoax,* exposes the academic decline of secular education. Copperman writes:

> I have recently met high-school graduates in San Francisco who did not know where the Pacific Ocean was, or whether New York was east or west of California, or how to spell the name of our country. Each year I meet dozens of parents who are shocked to discover that their children read three, four, or five years below their level.

Parents who send their youngsters to Christian schools will spend less than one-third the total of educating a public school student for their children's tuition and registration fees. The current twelve-year total for educating a Christian school student is $11,400. This figure includes average tuition costs and $1,300 for registration fees and books. In addition to spending less than one-third the cost the taxpayers pay for a public school education, parents of Christian school students will receive more in quality instruction. The standardized test scores of Christian school students indicate they are significantly ahead of their public school counterparts. The latest results of the Stanford Test of Academic Skills administered to thousands of Christian school students indicate that first graders in Christian schools are nine months ahead of the national average. Eighth graders are twelve months ahead.

Christian school students have not totally arrived academically, but it is clear that youngsters who are educated in Christian schools do not pay an academic penalty to receive a Christian education.

The Impact of Humanism in the Public Schools

Mel and Norma Gabler are two of the most remarkable people I have ever met. Nineteen years ago, they became concerned about the content of a textbook that their son brought home from his Texas public school. As Christians who felt a responsibility for what their children were taught, they complained to the teacher and administration. They were told to complain to the State Textbook Adoption Committee in Austin, Texas, the state capital. Mel Gabler wrote their complaint in the legal format required and Norma presented their case to the committee. Much to their amazement, they won! The textbook was taken off the official adoption list for the state of Texas. This was just the beginning for the Gablers. Since that beginning in 1961, they have become the nation's leading textbook evaluators. The walls of their home in Longview, Texas, are lined with textbooks. They are well known to every textbook publisher in the United States. They have been featured on local and national television and in national periodicals. They have spoken at Christian school conventions and are now strong advocates of Christian schools.

The Gablers have been instrumental in improving many textbooks. They will be the first to tell you, however, that there is such a flood tide of humanistic influence among American textbook publishers and in public school curriculum manuals that there is little hope of turning the system around.

The digression from Bible-oriented textbooks to humanistic textbooks has not happened overnight. It has been a gradual process. In his monograph on "While Men Slept," Dr. Donald Boys wrote:

> Spending an afternoon with books used by the early American schools is an exciting discovery. In every subject the Bible was the only reliable authority for the right answers and the right way to live. In 1800 the Bible or moral lessons consisted of 99 percent of the material, but by 1875 the moral and spiritual content had been slashed 50 percent. By 1946 less than 1 percent of the readers in Massachusetts had any moral or biblical content! . . . Our present texts are riddled with sex, vulgarity, and violence. They are anti-American, anti-free enterprise and anti-parents. They are crude, depressing, and filled with inaccuracies—the result of a strange religion known as Secular Humanism. Humanism teaches that there are no absolute answers, so anything is acceptable.

I define a humanist as a man-centered person who attributes all things to man and a Christian as one who is God-centered and attributes all things to God. There is a battle raging between these two forces, both competing for your child's mind, heart, and soul. The forces of Satan in recent years have taken on a unique form of religious overtones. In other words, atheistic humanism has become a religion. It was officially recognized as such in 1961 in the Torcaso vs. Watkins decision before the U.S. Supreme Court. Representing seven of the nine justices, Justice Black wrote:

> Among religions in this country which do not teach what would generally be considered a belief in the existence of God are Buddhism, Taoism, Ethical Culture, *Secular Humanism* and others.

The decline of American textbooks has paralleled the rise of secular humanism as a recognized religion. The Pro-Media Foundation Leaflet No. 279, entitled, "What is Humanism," reported the following:

> Since 1876, advocates of Humanism have organized themselves into an atheistic, secular religion called Humanism, and now seek to enforce their atheistic religion upon all peoples, in a new world order. . . .
>
> Humanism involves a multitude of small and large organizations, each claiming budget difficulties. However the overall impact of these "independently acting" groups convinces the informed observer that practically unlimited funds are available for Humanism's projects.
>
> Although this religion is embraced by a small minority, the financing behind Humanism is formidable. The thrust of Humanism expansion is far less by persuasion than by seeking to convert Humanistic philosophies into public laws and school curricula which—unless they are vigorously contested and defeated—will soon control the minds and the actions of all other citizens, in a new state religion.

John Dewey, father of American "progressive" education, was an atheist and a card-carrying humanist. In 1933, he signed the Humanist Manifesto I, and he was a charter member of the American Humanist Association. Because of the strong influence of John Dewey, many of America's public school educators followed Dewey into humanism. What does a humanist believe? The typical humanist attitude is expressed in the creed from the British Humanist Association:

> I believe in no God and no hereafter. It is immoral to indoctrinate children with such beliefs. Schools have no right to do so, nor indeed, have parents. I believe that religious education and prayers in school should be eliminated. . . . I believe that denominational schools should be abolished. . . . I believe that children should be taught religion as a matter of historical interest, but should be taught about all religions including HUMANISM, MARXISM, MAOISM, COMMUNISM, and other attitudes of life. They must be taught the objections to religion. I believe in a non-religious social morality.

Humanism is being taught in public schools and in a few liberal private schools in the form of value clarification, sex education, family living, and environmental studies. Dr. Sidney Simon, author of *Values Clarification*, explained in an article in the "Florida Pupil Quarterly" that values clarification is a method for teachers to change the values of children "without getting caught!"

Public education operates from at least eight humanistic premises:

- Man is supreme.
- Man is inherently good.
- Man is an animal.
- Man evolved from lower forms of life.
- Common practice sets the standard.
- Bad environment is to blame for evil.
- Criminals are merely antisocial.
- The term "maladjustment" explains all adverse human behavior.

Christians often sing a beautiful song entitled, "He is Lord." When they sing, "He is Lord," they are, of course, referring to God—not to man. To the Christian, God is supreme—not man.

The humanists within the public school system deny that God exists, that God created the earth, that man has a soul, or that he needs a Savior. The humanists believe in group morality, individual morality, almost any kind of morality except Bible morality. They say that lawbreakers have a social adjustment problem but they are not sinners, and that there is no need for guilt feelings because they are not responsible for their actions.

These humanistic doctrines are held to be true by a majority of public school teachers. They acquired their humanistic, religious philosophies in the government's "seminaries" known as state colleges and universities and a few private institutions. They carry their humanistic beliefs into their classrooms and their curriculum and slowly filter it into the minds of their students.

Humanistic educators are not moved by the fact that taxpayers will spend $144 billion on public education this year, yet Scholastic Aptitude Test scores plummet. Their primary concern is not teaching basic skills but teaching "social change." They picture themselves as "change agents" rather than teachers imparting skills and wisdom to the next generation.

Humanistic educators are not friends of Christianity, of Christian parents, or of the church. They believe children belong to the world. Their objective is to wean children away from their parents and to make them "world citizens"—subjects of the coming "one world government." Sounds incredible, doesn't it? But it's true! Were it not for the power of Christ, it would be frightening. If you are a believer in Jesus Christ, the following Scripture passage will be significant to you.

> Every spirit that confesseth not that Jesus Christ is come in the flesh is not of God: and this is that spirit of antichrist, whereof ye have heard that it should come; and even now already is it in the world. Ye are of God, little children, and have overcome them: because greater is he that is in you, than he that is in the world (1 John 4:3, 4).

Should Christians Send Their Children to Public Schools?

A few people out there still believe Christians should not "retreat" from the public schools—that Christian parents should risk the spiritual, social, and academic future of their own children to "save" the public school system. As Christian Americans, I believe we have an obligation to vote in elections for public school boards. Within the range of "responsible civic duty" Christians should attempt to improve the public system.

There is, however, an underlying problem in the public school system that a whole city of Christian voters could not change, and it is still a fundamental reason why Christians should not send their children to the public school. It's the philosophy! The underlying philosophy of the public school is secular humanism. A Christian teacher in an otherwise "ideal" public school cannot hold before her students an open Bible and say, "All truth is God's truth." The only position she can represent within the confines of public school philosophy is "truth is limited to the human intellect." Humanism and Christianity are diametrically opposed. One believes in the supremacy of God, the other in the supremacy of man.

It is difficult for Christian Americans to understand how devastating humanism really is. It is equally difficult for many people to believe that humanism is a religion, and that it is the official religion of America's public school system.

The name "public school" is confusing. It would help considerably if the public schools were named according to their philosophic position. For example, they might be called "Man-

Centered Schools" or "Humanistic School No. 433." If public schools were named according to their philosophic premise rather than by their source of financial support—the taxpaying public—it would open the eyes of many people.

Perhaps you are among those who believe that public schools are philosophically neutral. This is the popular view of most Americans. This, of course, is Biblically impossible. Jesus said, "He that is not with me is against me; and he that gathereth not with me scattereth abroad" (Matthew 12:30). Since public schools are not *for* Jesus Christ, then according to Jesus himself, they are *against* Him. It is difficult for me to believe that it is somehow Christ-honoring for Christians to send their God-given children to a school that is against Christ! There is no teaching in the Bible that justifies Christians sending their children to schools that are against Christ. In my view, it is sinful to do so.

A former public school administrator who wishes to remain anonymous wrote the following statement:

> The public schools increasingly are becoming militantly secular— beyond that envisioned by the Supreme Court in its decisions concerning the separation of church and state. Humanism is espoused actively, along with militant feminism. They promote relative morality, rebellion against authority, and sometimes weird and supernatural practices. The philosophers of the public schools have discovered that it is very difficult to teach children in a vacuum. So they have turned their emphasis away from traditional subject matter toward various schemes for perfecting society and individuals. I know for a fact that children from kindergarten through high school are propagandized concerning one or more of the above mentioned concepts.

Max Rafferty, former superintendent of public schools in California, wrote in one of his nationally syndicated columns:

> Horrors! I mean, who really knows what's right or wrong these days? The schools are currently teaching mostly "situation ethics," or "what's good for the cannibal is bad for the missionary." How can a teacher possibly tell students that certain things are eternally and damnably wrong? I know Jesus Christ did, but He wouldn't be allowed even to open His mouth in a public school classroom today.

Is it correct for Christians to send their children to public schools? I see no justification for doing so in Scripture, nor do I believe that good sound judgment would permit it.

The modern Christian school movement is a relatively new phenomenon. As is the case with all institutions established by mortals, there are areas that need improvement. But the Christian school movement is here to stay. It has enormous momentum. It will become many times larger than it is today. Some Christians have been hesitant to accept the concept of weekday schools in their churches. They forget that for two hundred years before the development of public schools, nearly all schools in America were Christian schools housed in church buildings. Most often, the teachers were church pastors. Christian schools are not a return to those harsh schools, but they are a return to a Bible-centered educational philosophy and to some academic basics that offer great promise for America.

PART TWO

THE FAMILY

Keeping the Family Strong

by Phyllis Schlafly

Today's unprecedented rates of divorces, illegitimate births, abortions, teenage pregnancies, venereal disease, homosexuality, and unwed couples cohabiting make it clear that the institution of the family is under severe attack. Added to this list of rampant sin, there is the added danger of an anti-family ideology.

The 1980 White House Conference on Families pitted two contrary ideologies against each other: (1) those who believe that a family is a group of people bound together by blood, marriage or adoption; and (2) those who want to redefine marriage to include any group of people with common interests who live together, regardless of whether the liaison is moral or immoral.

Much has been written about the various causes of the current attacks on the moral, the social, and the economic integrity of the family unit, but one major cause is often omitted from the list—the women's liberation movement. Yet it is vitally important for Christians to examine its anti-family ideology and effect.

Women's lib is a disease—a widespread, highly contagious psychological disease. Women's lib induces young women to reject marriage and motherhood. It persuades middle-aged women to walk out on their families, even when the usual breakup causes—adultery, alcohol, or money problems—do not exist.

Here are a few examples of the problems I find every week on college campuses. A young man comes to me for counseling. He loves and wants to marry a young woman completing her graduate degree. She tells him frankly that she doesn't care to have any children and, if she does, she doesn't plan to take care of the baby, who can be put in a child care center at the age of three weeks. She doesn't plan on letting anything interfere with her career. What should he do?

A college woman asks me, "What can you tell me to tell my mother who has raised four children but now thinks her whole life has been wasted because she hasn't been anything except a homemaker?"

Some college men are inordinately interested in the subject of women's liberation. Why? It turns out that their mothers one day just walked out on their husbands and teenage children—no reason; they just said they wanted to seek their own fulfillment. It seems to matter not whether the family was northern and liberal or southern and conservative.

These examples are just some of the evidences of the disease of women's liberation, which brings about a psychological brainwashing of its victims. To the young woman, women's lib says, "When you wake up in the morning, the cards are stacked against you. You'll never get a good job, and, if you do, you won't be paid or promoted as you should be, because society discriminates against women. If you get married, your husband will treat you like a servant, and life is nothing but dirty dishes and diapers. The home is a prison. Women are second-class citizens; they live in serfdom; women are not even persons under the United States Constitution."

To the middle-aged wife, women's lib says, "You poor wretch! You've lived for twenty years under a man's name! How could you endure such an indignity! All your labors are worthless because you haven't been paid a cash wage. You should take back your own name, establish your independent life, and seek your own identity." And so the wives walk out on husbands and children, seeking liberation from home, husband, family.

No wonder the devotees of women's lib have psychological problems! Women's lib gives women a negative outlook on life. This chip-on-the-shoulder attitude makes it very difficult to have a positive attitude toward husband, children, family, or country.

After putting down women in this negative ideology, and making a wife feel that her life has been wasted, women's lib offers the "solution:" Seek your *own* fulfillment over every other value.

Women's lib is thus part of the new narcissism of the 1970's. Narcissus was the famous youth of Greek mythology who fell in love with his own image in a reflecting pool. Women's lib turns a woman inward to satisfy her own desires as the supreme goal in life.

Thus women's lib is a part of the "Me Generation," based on achieving a selfish goal as recompense for past grievances—some real, some manufactured, all exaggerated. Like every revolutionary movement, women's lib has identified some genuine grievances and created others. It has cultivated all wrongs, real and imagined, and made them grow bigger. An artificial environment in which such grievances grow like Jack's beanstalk is the "consciousness-raising session" where bitter women eagerly exchange horror stories about how some men have mistreated them.

The consciousness-raising sessions produce Typhoid Marys carrying the disease of women's lib, which in turn produces marriage breakups among middle-aged couples, teenagers abandoned while they most need the security of a stable family, and a flight from motherhood, a far-reaching social phenomenon. The decline in the American birth rate is already producing tremendous social and economic consequences. The killing of their unborn babies by more than a million American mothers every year is a virulent moral cancer. Worst of all for the moral vitality of the next generation is the conscious decision of so many mothers (including college-educated women) to forsake the duty of mothering the babies they bear by delegating that duty to a hired surrogate or to a child-care institution.

The ideology of women's lib is based on four fundamental dogmas. First, women have been oppressed through the centuries, kept down in a kind of serfdom. The United States Constitution and Christianity are two of women's oppressors, and women are equally mistreated in the American/Judeo-Christian civilization and the rest of the world.

Second, the greatest oppression of women is that they get pregnant and have babies, so society must make women equal to men in their right *not* to be pregnant. Hence, the women's liberationists are oriented to abortion-on-demand, financed by the government, taught in schools as no more serious than a tonsillectomy, and mandated in all hospitals, public or private.

Third, it is unfair that society expects mothers to care for their babies. This stereotyped expectation of society discriminates against women by relegating them to the confining, menial task of caring for babies within the domestic prison. So women must be liberated by the establishment of child-care institutions, universally available for all socio-economic classes, financed by the taxpayers, so that mothers can achieve their full equality in the work force with fathers.

Fourth, there really isn't any difference between the sexes (except certain biological organs), and all those other differences you *think* you see are due merely to sex-stereotyped education and centuries of discrimination against women. Thus, many college women I meet on the campuses every week really believe that the only reason girls can't play football equally with boys is that girls' sports haven't had as much funding as boys' sports.

To remedy what they believe is sex discrimination, the women's lib advocates have set out to build a gender-free world in which women and men are always treated exactly alike. There are to be no more husbands and wives, only spouses; no more mothers and fathers, only parents; no more boys and girls, only students and athletes. There are to be no more "sex stereotypes." Basically, this is an ideology based on the premise that God goofed in making humans of two different kinds, and we should remedy His mistake by constitutional and legislative means.

The fallacies in the dogmas of women's lib should be obvious to all who believe that God knew what He was doing when He created men and women with different bodies, different responsibilities, and different missions, and when He furthermore ordained their harmonious living together in the family as the basic unit in society, and as the nest in which the next generation can be nurtured and taught to know God's love and God's laws. Christian mothers look upon the ability to participate in the creation of human life as God's great gift to women, and the ability to care for their babies in their own home as one of the great benefits of the American social and legal system, which accords preeminent rights to the family.

Just as the Christian belief in God's Word and in the eternal validity of the Ten Commandments, the ideology of women's liberation has developed its own commandments. Only by understanding those false statements can we understand the fruit of the poisoned tree and innoculate ourselves against it.

The first commandment is that a gender-free rule must be applied to every federal and state law, bureaucratic regulation, educational institution, textbook, and expenditure of public funds. Males and females must have identical treatment always. Gender must never be a basis for deciding anything. Thus, young women must be drafted and assigned to military combat duty when young men are. A husband's duty to support his wife cannot be greater than a wife's duty to support her husband. All-girls' and all-boys' schools and colleges must be forbidden because they sexually discriminate.

The second commandment is that society must seek equality between the sexes even at the expense of justice. In a just society organized under the Judeo-Christian ethic, the total of the rights and responsibilities of men can be balanced equally with those of women. Not so in the world of women's liberation. The ideology demands equality of *every* right and *every* responsibility. Since there is no way to legislatively equalize the differences between men and women put there by God, injustice and irrationality result from the artificial equality that a sex-neutral rule imposes.

The third commandment of women's liberation is that women must be given the benefit of reverse discrimination in the job market in order that female quotas can be achieved for all job categories. In addition to the obvious injustice of this rule, it constitutes an attack on the economic integrity of the family unit because the wife, who is the second wage-earner in the family, receives preferential employment and promotion preference over the husband, who is trying principally to support his wife and family. The result is to penalize the traditional family and to drive more and more wives out of the home.

The fourth commandment of women's liberation is that uniformity should replace diversity, and thus all remaining aspects of our life should be federalized. For every problem that the family faces today, women's liberation offers only one solution: another bureau and the expenditure of more federal tax dollars. There is no evidence to prove that Washington, D.C., is the fountainhead of all wisdom. In fact, many Washington, D.C. bureaucrats are part of the problem.

The drive for federal child care is a major feature of this effort toward federalization. Christians believe that parents have the responsibility for the care and upbringing of their children, not the federal government.

The fifth commandment of women's liberation is that we must be as neutral between morality and immorality as between the institution of the family and alternate lifestyles. Thus, prostitutes and lesbians must be treated with the same dignity as wives; homosexuals the same as heterosexuals; mothers who kill their unborn babies the same as those who give birth to their babies. The women's lib advocates ignore the tragic consequences to individuals and to society, forgetting that "righteousness exalteth a nation, but sin is a reproach to any people."

The women's lib movement and the federal bureaucrats have worked for years on a plan that would drive wives and mothers out of the home and into the work force. The plan would provide financial incentives for women to abandon full-time care of their children, even when very young. It calls for a drastic restructuring of the Social Security system by eliminating the 40-year-old policy of protecting the traditional family and replacing it with a policy that would induce divorce.

The anti-family plan was set forth by the Department of Health, Education and Welfare in a 1979 report called "Social Security and the Changing Roles of Men and Women." This report presents several "options," all of which discriminate against the traditional family. These "options" would eliminate the homemaker's present benefits (the dependent spouse's benefits), which are the benefits a housewife now receives after retirement, based on her husband's earnings. Under the proposed changes, the traditional family would *either* be cut 19 percent in benefits after retirement *or* be charged about double in payroll taxes paid before retirement.

These proposed changes, if enacted, would artifically induce millions of homemakers to enter the labor force in order to provide for their own economic security or to pay the new expensive Homemaker's Tax.

This is just one example of the anti-family legislative proposals that are promoted by the women's lib advocates in Congress and by such federally-funded lib groups as the Commission on International Women's Year.

When the women's liberation advocates started their activities in the 1960's, they were a small, strident group. Today, they are still a small, strident group, but most of them are on the payroll of some government agency or in the media, so they can work for their goals on our money. As a result, they have brought about tremendous changes in our educational system, our laws, our armed services, our labor force, and our social structure.

Fortunately, they have not been successful in their major goal: changing the United States Constitution by passing the Equal Rights Amendment. If ever ratified, ERA would give them the totally gender-free society achieved through total federal control.

ERA would throw a monkey wrench into God's distribution of responsibilities between men and women, and into His plan for the social and moral integrity of the family unit. ERA would throw a monkey wrench into the unique American constitutional system of division of powers between the federal government and the states by concentrating practically all power in Washington. ERA would, for example, give the federal government new powers over private schools, even if they receive no public money. ERA would destroy the military defense of the United States and promote immorality by imposing the commandments of women's liberation on the armed forces.

The time is past when Christian families can ignore the assault being waged by government employees through legislative lobbying and control of the public schools. "When the righteous are in authority, the people rejoice: but when the wicked beareth rule, the people mourn."

God has blessed the American people with more spiritual and material blessings than any nation in the history of the world. We have an obligation to preserve that heritage for our children. We default in this responsibility if we let a strident anti-family group sabotage our heritage. We should "be strong in the Lord, and in the power of his might. Put on the whole armor of God that you may be able to stand against the wiles of the devil." And we should—must—be doers of the word, not hearers only. The survival of the family depends on it.

Abortion and Euthanasia

by Dr. C. Everett Koop

Twenty-five years ago—perhaps even ten—any discussion of biomedical ethics would have been based upon absolutes of right and wrong. The sanctity of human life would have been defended within the framework of our Judeo-Christian heritage. But in medicine as in other disciplines, situational ethics now provides the framework in a new secular humanism.

Beginning in the late 1960's and early 1970's, a number of forces at work in our own country as well as abroad laid the foundation for human behavior against a background of moral decay, where life other than one's own is lightly esteemed and readily destroyed. They had circulated false figures in reference to criminal abortion-related deaths; they exaggerated the population problem.[1] No one has said it better or more succinctly than Dr. Joseph Stanton of Boston:

> In the confluence of women's liberation, sexual freedom, and the concern for ecology, population, and pollution, vast forces inimicable to the wellbeing of human embryo and fetus were set in motion. The American Law Institute was profferring some reasonable liberalization of the abortion laws to take care of the so-called hard cases—physical and mental health, incest, rape and genetic defect. The "quality of human life" ethic gained respectability at the expense of human life itself in socially and academically impeccable circles. As medical indications for abortion evaporated, doctors increasingly invoked mental

health as justification for abortion. Undocumented statements subsequently acknowledged as unfounded in truth were endlessly repeated until they acquired the ring of truth. Sincere and concerned people were disturbed. They were purposely and purposefully misled. Thousands of women were said to be dying each year at the hands of criminal abortionists. Some estimated 10,000 women died each year of illegal abortions; others said 5,000. Obviously, inflation hit the abortion statistics before it hit the grocery shelf.[2]

In 1973, not by any legislative act, but on the basis of two Supreme Court decisions (Rowe v. Wade and Doe v. Bolton) abortion-on-demand became the law of the land by eliminating the personhood of the unborn child and declaring that the decision for abortion was in the realm of privacy between a woman and her physician.

The Supreme Court rulings went far beyond even the most optimistic hopes of the pro-abortionist elite. It was hoped in some quarters that the American moral outrage concerning these two Supreme Court decisions in January of 1973 might lead the Supreme Court in subsequent actions to pull back from their hard-nosed position established in Rowe v. Wade. Such was not the case, however.

In 1973 Justice Blackmun wrote the majority opinion of the Supreme Court decision. He said that once the fetus was viable— that is, able to exist on its own outside the womb—the state could regulate or even prohibit abortion. Subsequently, the Commonwealth of Pennsylvania legislature passed a law requiring that if the victim of an intended abortion might be viable, the doctor must use that abortion technique "which would provide the best opportunity for the fetus to be aborted alive." This law was struck down, however, by the Supreme Court in January of 1979, with Justice Blackmun saying that the state of Pennsylvania had taken that invitation too far.

In July of 1979 the Supreme Court declared unconstitutional a Massachusetts law that required unmarried minor girls to get the approval of their parents before obtaining a legal abortion. Said the Court on that occasion: "Every minor must have the opportunity—if she so desires—to go directly to a court without first consulting and notifying her parents." Justice Byron White, who showed his integrity in 1973 by dissenting from the majority opinion in Rowe v. Wade, had this to say about the Supreme Court's Massachusetts decision: "The Court now holds it unconstitutional for a state to require that in all cases parents receive notice that their daughter seeks an abortion and, if they object to the abortion, an opportunity to participate in a hearing that will determine whether it is in the best interest of the child to undergo the surgery.''

Forget the ethics of abortion, but consider what the decision does concerning the rights of parents or the relationship of parents to their children. The decision is a devastating blow at the integrity of the family.

Consider also the anti-family forces at work in denying the father of an unborn child any role in the decision for abortion made by the mother-to-be.

Anything that cheapens life undermines the family. Life became cheap in America when the Supreme Court found that our Constitution could permit abortion-on-demand. By September 1979—just six-and-a-half years after the decision, abortion at whim was urged as an ethical norm by HEW's ethicist, John Fletcher. I am referring to the new ethical norm of aborting an unborn child because it is not the sex the parents (mother) want.

When Justice Blackmun wrote the majority opinion in the 1973 rulings concerning abortion, he made it clear that if any religion was to be a guide to him in the decision-making process it would be paganism. He ignored the ethic of our Judeo-Christian heritage, but alluded to the practice of the ancient Persians, Greeks, and Romans. (He also ignored the Hippocratic tradition that has governed the practice of medicine in the United States since its inception—a tradition that specifically prohibits abortion.) It did not take obscure powers of prophecy to predict that born life would soon be in jeopardy: although the Persians, the Greeks, and the Romans practiced abortion, it was infanticide and euthanasia that are remembered as their inhumanities.

By making abortion-on-demand the law of the land, the Supreme Court set the stage for infanticide and euthanasia: first the unborn were deprived of their right to life, then the recently born were classified as having no potential for meaningful life.

One of the hallmarks of our culture today is the rapidity with which eras change. In looking pessimistically at the future in 1973, I saw infanticide being practiced openly within the decade. The change took place far faster than that, however. In 1972 the Johns Hopkins Hospital and Medical School produced a documentary film, "Who Shall Survive?" in which a newborn infant with

Down's syndrome (mongolism) was permitted to die by "inattention" when it was found that the infant also suffered from an intestinal obstruction easily correctable by surgery.

In 1973, eight months after the Supreme Court decisions on abortion, Duff and Campbell, writing in the *New England Journal of Medicine* concerning "Moral and Ethical Dilemmas in the Special Care Nursery," acknowledged that out of 299 babies who died in the previous two and a half years, 43 of them had been allowed to die after the physician had discussed with the family the propriety of not letting the child live.[3] It all starts with the concept that there is such a thing as life not worthy to be lived.

In 1977 the response of over 250 pediatric surgeons to a questionnaire centered around which surgical newborns should be treated and which should be allowed to die demonstrated the arbitrary base upon which such decisions are made.[4] If there is any segment of our culture that should understand what can be accomplished in the rehabilitative process of youngsters born with major defects, it is pediatric surgeons.

Since infanticide is homicide and since all who practice it should be prosecuted, it is called "selection"—selection of some newborn babies to life and selection of others to death—usually by starvation (which to the surprise of many takes several weeks).

Infanticide is nothing more than euthanasia of the newly born. The next category of citizens in our country who might be classed as individuals having life not worthy to be lived is the elderly.

Euthanasia is the purposeful killing of a dependent human being, allegedly for his own good. Whether this death is accomplished by passive means such as withholding vital support or a direct action to terminate a life makes no difference; in either instance a life is terminated. The result of the euthanasia movement could well be an emphasis that shifts from the killing of an individual for the alleged benefit of that individual to the killing of an individual for the benefit of others.

Advocates of euthanasia use as an example a dying patient who suffers an inordinate amount of pain from cancer and is beyond corrective measures. In this age with our ability to control pain and with our pharmacological knowledge of sedatives and pain killers, there is no need for that either/or type of philosophy. The hospice movement, long established in Europe, is a relatively recent import to the United States. Hospice cases have shown that when the patient who has a painful terminal illness receives proper physical, emotional, and spiritual support, his pain is reduced and total freedom from pain becomes achievable.

It is with terms such as the "right to die," "natural death," and "death with dignity" that the basic tenets of euthanasia are introduced. In any relationship between a physician and a patient, the patient is master and the physician is servant. When medicine is practiced in the realm of trust between patient and physician, the patient can count upon his physician to do the "right" thing. By the right thing, I mean not prolonging the act of dying, but giving the patient the full benefit of the life to which he is entitled.[5] [6]

The three inhumanities under discussion—abortion, infanticide, and euthanasia—might be likened to falling dominoes. The first domino to fall was abortion-on-demand, and it fell with a loud thud. Nothing has split our society as abortion has since the days of the practice of slavery, which took a civil war to overcome.

The second domino to fall was infanticide. It fell rather silently because, if you do not have intimate knowledge of the workings of an intensive care unit for newborns, you would never know about infanticide. It is practiced behind the shielding facade of a hospital. The third tottering domino is euthanasia. In any discussion of these three inhumanities, abortion is the pivotal issue.

A number of forces at work in America today are anti-family. The climbing divorce rate, the gay pride movement, extreme forms of women's lib, abortion-on-demand, single parenthood, and the loosening of sexual morals are definitely anti-family.

Sexually permissive American lifestyles and the breakdown of the family demand abortion. Yet the availability of legal abortion contributes to the very changes in our sexual mores—truly a vicious cycle.

One child in six now lives in a single parent family. Of every eight women to whom a child is born, one is not married (this was one in twenty in 1960). The labor force now supports more than half of American married women with children between the ages of six and seventeen (double the 1948 statistics). A third of the women who are unmarried with children under three years of age are presently in the labor force.

Abortion, infanticide, and euthanasia are symptoms of a malady that affects our present-day American culture. Whereas once the consensus of this country was Judeo-Christian with the belief that every life was precious because it was made in the image of God, the consensus is now humanistic.

Humanism has several definitions, but the secular humanism I am talking about has become the secular religion of our times. When one views the universe as a mechanism, coming about without a creator, when the planet we live on is a great machine, when human beings themselves are machines—why should each human life be viewed as unique and precious?

The situation in America today represents the crossroads of the corruption of medicine with the corruption of law. That is a statement which should strike terror to the hearts of those who know history. It was the corruption of medicine, beginning with psychiatry in Germany in the 1930's that met the corruption of law at the crossroads. So-called mercy killing of insane and senile adults and retarded children was followed by the Holocaust. Some of the medical and legal attitudes that were dominant in the 1930's in Germany are in our society today.

Abortion-on-demand following the Supreme Court decisions of 1973 threw the whole question of the sanctity of human life into focus. Biblically, this concept begins in the Old Testament after Cain had killed Abel. God promised that if there were to be a blood feud, He would repay sevenfold. Shortly after that, the covenant established between God and Noah indicated that if a man sheds another man's blood, by man shall that individual's blood be shed. Then came the Ten Commandments, one of which was "Thou shalt not kill." Close examination of this in context reveals that the killing had nothing to do with manslaughter or with war; it had to do with murder.

In the 139th Psalm, David clearly establishes the individual creation of the individual person.

> You created my inmost being;
>   you knit me together in my mother's womb.
> I praise you because I am fearfully and wonderfully
>   made;
>   your works are wonderful,
>   I know that full well.
> My frame was not hidden from you
>   when I was made in the secret place.
> When I was woven together in the depths of the earth,
>   your eyes saw my unformed body.
> All the days ordained for me
>   were written in your book
>   before one of them came to be. (Psalm 139:13-16, *NIV*)

When God called Jeremiah to be a prophet, He said, "Before I formed you in the womb, I knew you; before you were born I set you apart; I appointed you as a prophet to the nations" (Jeremiah 1:5, NIV).

There seems little doubt that God knew us as individuals from before the foundation of the world.

The New Testament follows right along. Jesus said that He came to confirm the law, and certainly His teachings and that of the apostles follow the general theme that life is indeed precious to God. You and I as his stewards have no right to destroy it.

What are the Christian alternatives to the things discussed here? There are two general spheres of activity: educational-political and personal compassion. The first thing that the Christian must do is to be educated about the problems at hand. This means perhaps joining a pro-life group in order to understand the legal, social, theological, and practical aspects of these in-humanities. With such knowledge the Christian should then be politically active in casting his vote in elections for men and women who will uphold the sanctity of human life. Every effort must be bent to achieve an amendment to the Constitution guaranteeing the right to life of every unborn child.

On a personal basis (or speaking collectively in reference to the church) compassion for the woman who is pregnant and does not wish to be, compassion for the family who has a less-than-perfect child, and finally compassion for the elderly who feel abandoned by their families, are Christian imperatives. If the Christian church had been compassionate rather than judgmental, had pro-vided havens of refuge and had provided physical, emotional, psychological, and material help to those in distress, the inhuman trends in society under discussion might never have taken place. The Christian has to be willing to stand up and be counted. He certainly cannot play ostrich.

> Rescue those being led away to death;
>   hold back those staggering toward slaughter.
> If you say, "But we knew nothing about this,"
>   does not he who weighs the heart perceive it?
> Does not he who guards your life know it?
>   Will he not repay each person according to what he has
>   done?

(Proverbs 24:11, 12, NIV)

50

Scripture quotations in this chapter are from the *New International Version* of the Bible, © 1978, New York Bible Society International.

[1]Bernard Nathanson and Richard W. Ostling, *Aborting America* (New York: Doubleday, 1979).

[2]J. R. Stanton, "Abortion: Flawed Premise and Promise" (NSA, delivered many occasions).

[3]R. S. Duff and A. G. M. Campbell, "Moral and Ethical Dilemmas in the Special Care Nursery," *New England Journal of Medicine,* CCLXXXIX (1973), 890.

[4]A. Shaw, J. G. Randolph, and B. Manard, "Ethical Issues in Pediatric Surgery: A National Survey of Pediatricians and Pediatric Surgeons," *Journal of Pediatrics,* LX (1977), 588.

[5]C. E. Koop, *The Right to Live, the Right to Die* (Wheaton, Illinois: Tyndale, 1976).

[6]Francis A. Schaeffer and C. E. Koop, *Whatever Happened to the Human Race?* (Old Tappan, New Jersey: Revell, 1979).

Quality Living

by Jeanette Lockerbie

It was a hot California afternoon. With a friend, I was sunning on the deck of her condominium pool. From a lounge chair a few yards away I overheard, "*Rich.* What is 'rich'?" The speaker then answered his own question. "Peace of mind. *That's* what 'rich' is. That's what I would call *quality living.*"

A snippet of conversation, from a person whose face I didn't see, summed up his philosophy as to quality living.

Quality living. A high-sounding phrase beloved of the ad writers in the real estate business. What do the words connote?

Generally, they are bait, hooking the would-be home buyer with tacit promises such as *unusually desirable location, elite neighbors, extravagant acreage, exclusiveness*—whatever conjures up an image of quality living in the reader's mind.

Quality living, by definition, reflects the individual's background. In the material sense, the always affluent might take the good life as the norm, or they may scorn or repudiate their affluence. For the poor, a quest for quality living might kindle a lifelong relentless drive to become rich.

Whatever one's background or thinking, however, there are some things we cannot escape. One of these is *relationships.*

As long as two people are left on earth, how they relate to one another will play a large part in the quality of their lives. And the more persons who *are* a part of it—father, mother, brother, sister, husband, wife, son, daughter, grandparent, neighbor, employer, employee, pastor, church friend—whatever the connection, each one adds to the potential for god or bad relationships.

The Bible brings this matter of relationships down to two: a vertical relationship, "Thou shalt love the Lord thy God," and a horizontal relationship, "Love thy neighbor as thyself" (Matthew 22:37-39). God makes no place for the nit-picking question, "Who is thy neighbor?"

Admittedly, God has made us with all the weaknesses that flesh is heir to. Nevertheless, He does not issue impossible commands. He has bidden us to "Be kind," "Love one another," "Be tenderhearted and forgive one another." These virtues will contribute to and enhance the very best of interpersonal relationships. We are constantly challenged by the Word of God and prompted by the indwelling Holy Spirit to strive to "live peaceably with all men" (Romans 12:18).

Quality living encompasses a broad range of thought, feeling and experience. I've therefore sampled people from various professional, economic, and geographic backgrounds, asking "What, in your opinion, is quality living?"

A consensus of their replies:

Contentment

An optimistic outlook on life

Complete reliance on God

Getting your heart's desires

None of those I interviewed felt he had truly achieved this level of living; he was stating a goal.

Significantly, health was rarely mentioned (maybe I queried healthy friends). Nor were the prevailing issues such as smog, water pollution, or—a big concern in my area—earthquakes. Three of the four definitions are inner; only the fourth—Getting your heart's desire—has outer connotations. Similarly, when heading a convention billed as "Psychology for Non-Psychologists," Dr. John A. Brabel said, "There is a lot of talk about the quality of life here in San Diego and most of it has to do with our external environment. But the quality of life can also be enhanced by improving our private, inner environment."

Contentment

The one who views quality living as contentment has undoubtedly worked on his inner environment.

"Contented as a kitten," we often say. But not all kittens are contented—else why do they meow? The "contented" image is that of a fat, furry ball purring its satisfaction with its circumstances, its every want met by a doting owner.

How many people do you know who figuratively purr with content?

According to the noted Henry Ward Beecher, "We see in a lifetime only a dozen or so faces marked by the peace of a contented spirit."

In our frenzied times the figure may be smaller.

Not one of us is born contented. A baby's first cry signals that he is not quite happy with this new scene. This is but the beginning of a lifelong quest for contentment. The same is true for Christian and non-Christian alike.

The Bible teaches that contentment, like the taste for olives, is a learned response. Paul makes it amply clear that he was not always the serene saint. "I have learned," he wrote, "in whatsoever state I am, therewith to be content" (Philippians 4:11). Contentment does not come naturally to most of us. But we can *learn*.

Some people *do* learn life's lessons more quickly than others, thus saving themselves a world of frustration. As in all phases of learning there has to be (1) a willingness to be taught; (2) access to the resources for learning; and (3) a good teacher, or a right model to emulate. One such model comes to my mind. She was unfailingly serene; not smug, not pious. She was elderly. I was privileged to get to know her when I was young and a new Christian. I loved her as did my new Christian friends and we all learned from her. The secret of her deep well of contentment was best expressed in what we came to call "Mother Young's hymn"—"*I have Christ; what want I more?*"

Others of us fuss and fume, or whimper at "fate." And meanwhile we make cosmetic manufacturers rich as we seek to erase frown lines from our faces. How much better to take to heart this Biblical equation:

Godliness + contentment = great gain (1 Timothy 6:6).

A major factor in contentment is valuing today for itself. All too often we are either yesterday- or tomorrow-oriented. Nothing is wrong with saving for a rainy day, but not to such an extent that we can't enjoy fine weather when it comes!

I know of Christians who say, "If I only knew how long I'm to live, I would know how much to give to God's work today." Then they give so little that they miss God's special blessing for the cheerful giver.

Undue dwelling on past or future is at the expense of today. Is today—*now*—so hard to live with?

The only resources promised us come to us by the day. We did not receive a holdover supply yesterday, nor can we draw on tomorrow's portion. In this enjoy-it-today-pay-for-it-tomorrow society, many would wish to mortgage tomorrow's strength. God is too wise to grant us such an option.

Yesterday? We can learn from it. But we cannot call back an ounce of its allotted strength. As for tomorrow, our Lord bade us, "Take therefore no thought for the morrow" (Matthew 6:34).

We can all say, *Today* is mine. What we do with it determines our satisfaction with the present.

Sometimes I ponder how we influence a child's thinking when we place undue emphasis on "tomorrow." Our input, "Not now, Johnny—when you're older you can do that," tends to make today just a stepping stone to a happier time, discounting it as valuable for itself. I can still in memory see my grandmother shaking her head at me as I would wish out loud for tomorrow, my birthday, or Christmas. "Child," she would say, "you're just wishing your life away."

In the light of these beliefs, what I am about to say may *seem* totally contradictory. But it is not.

An Optimistic Outlook on Life

In order to maintain a good degree of emotional health, we need the balance of both a realistic appreciation of today and good feelings about tomorrow.

I have long been influenced by something I heard an eminently successful Christian executive say. With a merry twinkle in his eyes he quipped, "I can hardly wait to get up in the morning to see what God is up to." No morning person myself, I could yet grasp what this man was sharing. His own *good expectations* reflected his assurance that God *is* involved with the affairs of men in His universe.

Some people, by contrast, appear to have made a life commitment to pessimism. It's thus important to keep in mind that both optimism and pessimism are highly contagious. We are almost always influencing *someone;* we can be a constructive or a destructive force in their lives as they can likewise be in ours.

Some time ago an article I wrote called "According to Your Expectations Be It Unto You," fell into the hands of a young mother. Later, following a Mother and Daughter Banquet at which I was the speaker, she shared this with me, to my delight: "I had always been a crepe hanger, always expected the worst to happen. I saw not the donut, I just saw the hole." Then her face brightened and she said, "That article was just for me. I began to ask the Lord to help me *specifically* to look for the good. It's taken time and I still have a ways to go, but I do find myself looking for something to *like* about a person or a thing."

What a joy to know that with God's help *we can change.*

No one need continue to live with what psychologists dub "catastrophic expectations." I know. I used to be a classic pessimist. I look back and see how I robbed myself of the happiness that good expectations can bring. And some of my poor attitudes must have rubbed off on my family and others around me. That explains something my son, Bruce, said to me a few years back, "Mother, I see you as a far better person than you ever were." High praise indeed from one's own loving son! A chunk of quality living at its best.

To the dedicated pessimist who is a believer in Christ, may I suggest that you saturate yourself in such verses as, "My God shall supply all your need according to his riches in glory in Christ Jesus" (Philippians 4:19). Note, please: not "according to your poor expectations." Also, "I will never leave thee nor forsake thee" (Hebrews 13:5). You don't have to go it alone. I've also heard many a Bible teacher assure his audience that the Bible gives 366 references to "Fear not . . ." (that's one for every day of the year and an extra for Leap Year!)

Quality living is always relative. I've seen a rare quality of life in a Bangladesh village where the people seem to have nothing. The women may have only the sari they are wearing. The furnishings of their bamboo thatch homes are a bed, and frequently not even one chair. Yet I've enjoyed immensely sitting with them, hearing them sing and seeing the shine in their beautiful dark eyes. They've shared without apology their meager food, and their compassion for one another. I will long remember, for instance, going "house calling" with Dr. Ralph Ankenman in such a Bengali village. The mother-in-law was the patient, and as I stood near enough to see, one daughter-in-law held the woman's hands, another daughter-in-law gently covered the patient's eyes so the frightened woman would not see the needle the doctor was about to insert. I thought—then and now—*These people have so little to give each other, but I have just witnessed a quality of caring we could well emulate in our dealings with hurting people.*

Complete Reliance on God

Here we arrive at a marriage of theology and practicality. Every person we might ask would conceivably express a different interpretation of "complete reliance on God."

"Relying on God *for what?*" one might question, while another would want to discuss the boundaries of such dependence: "to what extent do we rely on God?"

Whether or not we ever stop to analyze our own dependence on the Lord, we are dependent on Him. We rely on God to keep the sun, moon and stars in their places and on course. Another area of dependence is that God will keep His vow to Noah (Genesis 8:22), "While the earth remaineth, seedtime and harvest, and cold and heat, and summer and winter, and day and night shall not cease." Inherent in our trust in this promise is our often taken for granted, "Give us this day our daily bread."

In such practicalities, what place does faith really have?

So-called complete reliance on God can be merely a high-sounding phrase until and unless it is, as some express it, "fleshed out." As a mere concept for discussion and debate, "complete reliance on God" will never produce quality living.

Faith *in practice* is a key factor: believing that God means what His Word says, and acting on that premise. Take, for instance the familiar "Seek ye first the kingdom of God, and his righteousness; and all these things shall be added unto you" (Matthew 6:33). Do these words of our Lord have pragmatic meaning for today's Christian?

Some time ago I asked three women in my Bible class to share the best piece of advice they had ever been given. The first two made a worthwhile contribution to the class. But it was Lois, the youngest of the three, whose words have stayed with me.

"I lived with fear," she admitted to the class, then explained, "My husband is a well-trained and qualified engineer, but he is a diabetic. After his graduation a number of fine job offers came his way, but as soon as diabetes was mentioned, the doors closed. Even after he was finally employed, the fear was still present: *Frank will lose his job. We won't be able to make the payments on our nice little home. We won't be able to care properly for our children.* I was plagued by these uncertainties; my mind dwelled on all the dark possibilities. I knew no peace—Christian though I was—though we had a wonderful marriage. But one day a Christian neighbor stopped by and I unloaded my burden on her. She listened, then sat silent for a minute or two.

"Then, this neighbor said, 'Lois, let me pass along to you the best advice anybody ever gave me. I can't think of anything that will do more to calm and reassure you.' " With shining eyes Lois then shared Matthew 6:33, "Seek ye first the kingdom of God, . . . and all these things shall be added unto you."

"I began to take the verse literally, pleading 'Lord, I'm relying on you to help me overcome these fears, to cast my husband's health and our future on you.' Gradually, this changed pattern changed my life. No, it did not reverse my husband's diabetic condition. It did not put an unending deposit in our bank account. It gave no guarantee that the children or I would never be sick or injured. What it did program into my days was a bedrock trust in God. I also realized for the first time that when God said, 'Seek ye first the kingdom . . .' *it was for my good;* to teach me the rewards of simple obedience and faith." Lois would agree that *she* has found the secret of quality living.

Getting Our Heart's Desires

There seem to be two schools of thought on this topic.

Some Christians have never learned to view God as the giver of every good and perfect gift. Parents, other Christians, or "the church" have made God to appear as a divine spoilsport, as though "if it's enjoyable it must be sinful or at least not God's will." Everything in nature should teach us differently: the beauty, the variety God has created for our eyes and ears.

At the other end of the spectrum is the thinking of today's secularist, "If it feels good, do it." No matter that it may harm or offend another, or even dishonor one's family or God. Just follow the dictates of your appetite in everything.

So where is the middle ground, the quality living aspect of obtaining our heart's desires?

What about, "Delight thyself also in the Lord, and he shall give thee the desires of thine heart" (Psalm 37:4). It would be pretty hard to delight in the Lord while harboring desires that are totally foreign to His will!

Our motives need to be examined in the area of our desires: why do I want whatever it is? Sometimes a little self-examining will shed light on our motives.

A form of quality living much to be desired is the ability to live with oneself, with no nagging conscience, no guilt we can't take care of Scripturally. The snare for some of us is that we can become "more adjustable"—giving our conscience more leeway. The thing that once seemed incompatible with our Christian testimony can become acceptable as we lower our standards to meet society's. When we permit ourselves to do this, it's at the expense of the genuine quality living Christ reserves for those who hear His voice and follow no other.

Dreams, Goals, and Fulfillment

One direct route to quality living is finding out where your natural ability lies and majoring in it. Nothing is quite so fulfilling.

All too many people drag themselves to a job they despise. It brings them no personal satisfaction; little sense of worth and achievement.

Far from enjoying quality living, they feel trapped, disenchanted with life. I hear them say, "I give the best part of my week to this 'nothing' job. It's a drag; I can't wait for Friday."

This need not be so.

God has blessed each of us with at least one ability. We can all do *something* very well. And we do best that for which we have a natural bent. In turn, the success experiences make the task fulfilling: more, it's a *delight*.

Moreover, God will one day hold us accountable for what we have done with the abilities He has given us.

It pays to take steps to discover your abilities. One way is through professional testing. To quote Dr. Clyde Narramore, "Your natural abilities are God's suggestions for your life's work."

Almost certainly, you will find that the things you dream of doing "someday" are tied into your God-given talents. Turn the dreams into goals. Where possible, train in the direction of your natural ability. This, in time, will lead to great satisfaction, to true quality living.

What Quality Living Is Not

Frequently we can best define a positive by way of a negative.

Quality living is not, as masses of people have been led to believe in our day, getting one's way ninety-five percent of the time.

Demanding our own way is a childish trait, expected and tolerated, even while the parents gently guide the child into less self-centered channels. In the adult, always wanting our own way is a mark of immaturity, of non-growth.

We never quite grow out of being demanding creatures to *some* degree. But, just as nature wills and provides for a baby to grow up, so does God will that as Christians we mature. One mark that we are growing is graciously enduring the crossing of our will. Oh, we will regress at times, and this may surprise us. However, even these regressions give way to more maturity and quality living.

The Source of All Quality Living

To return to the poolside philosopher's "What is 'rich'?" and his personal conclusion that *quality living* is peace. Where can you find such peace? What is it?

Peace is not a what, it is a Who. Jesus Christ is our peace. Christ offers us *His* peace as a legacy to every believer. Paul speaks of this unique brand of peace as "peace that passes understanding" (Philippians 4:7) and assures us that it will "keep our hearts and minds. . . ." Keep from what? From the nagging anxieties and doubts that contribute to both emotional and physical ills. In many instances the peace of God is the only genuine lasting cure.

Jesus calls it "My peace." He holds the formula. His peace is free even though it cost "the blood of His cross" and it is available throughout the world. Why should anyone who hears His "Come unto me" live even one day without His matchless peace? This is true quality living—to know the peace of God, which passes all understanding. It's past understanding to our unsaved neighbors who look on in amazement because we can "take" what they know would devastate them. And one of our finest means of Christian witness is our resting in God's peace while personal turmoil and trauma would otherwise swamp us.

The Sting Is Gone

Because we are created for eternity, ultimately "peace" is in knowing no fear of death, being assured that the sting of death has been taken away. For, whether we be rich or poor, sick or healthy, famous or "nobodies," death, the leveler, awaits all unless Christ comes again in our time.

With the apostle Paul, the Christian can fling out the challenge, "O death, where is thy sting? O grave, where is thy victory?" (1 Corinthians 15:55) The seventeenth-century poet, John Donne, expressed the same thought in his *Death, Be Not Proud:*

Death, be not proud, though some have called thee
Mighty and dreadful, for, thou art not so; . . .
One short sleep past, we wake eternally,
And death shall be no more; death, thou shalt die.

The poet/philosopher spoke well and truly. Death shall die! But we will not!

When we draw that last breath on earth we can know (not hope, not guess) that all is well with our eternal soul; that we are not heading for some "great unknown."

How can we be so sure?

The same compassionate Savior who comforted His disciples with "My peace I leave with you" also promised "I go to prepare a place for you . . ." (John 14:2). Think of it! A specially prepared place, planned for us by Christ who was in on the plans for all of creation.

It has been many a year since I heard an old minister speculate, "God made 'the world and all that in it is' in six days. Jesus said, 'I go to prepare a place for you,' and He has been preparing it for nigh on to 2000 years. What kind of 'place' must He be making for those that love Him!"

Whatever form the "place" that Jesus is preparing will take, it will be just right. Jesus said to *individuals* that He was preparing a place for them—for you and me. It will be totally appropriate and satisfying to each one of us, for "Jesus doeth all things well."

Just being at home with the Lord will be the zenith of life.

Nevertheless, while we await that glad day, God would have us live life to its fullest, each day a sample of quality living.

Marriage

by Clyde M. Narramore

Several years ago I served as a consulting psychologist on the staff of the Los Angeles County Superintendent of Schools. In this position I traveled throughout the greater Los Angeles area, visiting and helping local schools. When making a call on an elementary school one day, a principal said, "Will you please go upstairs and see what you can do to help that fourth grade teacher? He brought nothing with him into the classroom."

As I turned to go, he cautioned, "Be sure you get the right room. We have two fourth grades up there. The other teacher is excellent. He brought so much with him."

That, I thought, not only applies to teaching. It's also true of *marriage.* Some people bring a wealth of assets into the marriage. But some bring almost nothing . . . nothing but hangups.

The partners in a marriage need to consider seriously, "What am I bringing into this marriage?" For, surely, the course of marriage will be set by the qualities and attributes each brings into the relationship, transferring what he or she is before marriage into their life together.

A marriage certificate is no warranty against problems, no guarantee that the couple will live happily ever after. The devastating divorce rate indicates that *you are likely to head for a divorce!* Statistics shout loud and clear the fact that your marriage may very well end in an angry divorce court, leaving you with a broken heart, a broken dream, and a broken personality. And to make matters worse, you'll probably drag your children with you.

But you *can* sidestep a lifetime of tragedy and you *can* also build the kind of marriage that God will shower with untold blessings. With mounting evidence of what causes an unhappy home, you need not stumble into marriage in the dark.

What, then, are some of the important factors you can bring to your marriage?

The *spiritual condition* of each of the partners is all-important. Godliness is the glue that holds a marriage together. This is more than knowing that the other is a believer in Christ; there should be agreement on serving Christ—and before marriage, as much as possible, a decision as to where and how you will serve.

But the one, single, most significant influence upon marriage is in *the realm of the spiritual*. This includes spiritual conversion, Christian growth and maturity, and unreserved commitment to Jesus Christ. I'm not talking about going to church or giving to the poor (although these are worthwhile).

Linda provides an example of spiritual conversion, growth, and commitment. In her second year of high school she attended a summer Bible conference for teenagers. At this conference she saw herself as a sinner, in need of forgiveness. She listened carefully to the challenges of the speakers. As she talked with her roommates, and read the Bible, she came to see that she was a sinner and completely without the Lord. Before the conference ended she surrendered her life to Christ. As a result, God's Holy Spirit invaded her very being. She accepted the invitation of John 3:16, "For God so loved the world, that he gave his only begotten son, that whosoever believeth in him should not perish, but have everlasting life." This eternal transaction gave her a new nature, as spoken of in 2 Corinthians 5:17: "Therefore if any man be in Christ, he is a new creature: old things are passed away; behold, all things are become new."

The acceptance of Christ as her personal Savior changed the direction of her life. Before that week at the conference, she was trying to manage her own life. She had her own goals. She had her own limited power. Now that she was under the control of Jesus Christ, she began to walk in a new direction. She began to submit daily to the Word of God and its teachings. She became sensitive to the Holy Spirit who was indwelling her.

And as Linda returned home from the conference, she sought

out a church that preached Jesus Christ and taught the Word. She became a dynamic, committed Christian, growing day by day. In one year's time you would hardly have recognized Linda; she was so wonderfully changed. Will Linda's spiritual conversion and dynamic growth someday affect her marriage? Indeed!

About two years earlier, Carl, a teenager in a nearby state, had trusted Christ as his personal Savior. The claims of Christ became strong upon his life. Before long he joined a group of dynamic young people who had weekly Bible studies and who witnessed freely to other young people about their Lord. More than anything else, Carl wanted to get an education and serve the Lord. In time Carl enrolled in a Christian college where he could receive a Christ-centered education.

During his junior year in college, he met Linda, who had been saved a few years before. They liked each other and often talked about how they wanted to serve Christ. They eventually fell in love and made plans for marriage. They both lived clean, godly lives. They had a knowledge of God's Word, and they both wanted to put Christ first in their lives.

Now, that Carl and Linda have been married several years, let's take a brief look at their marriage.

1. Because they had yielded their lives to the Lord, He did indeed direct in their marriage.

2. They both put Christ first in their marriage. He transcends even their love for each other.

3. They both have the same basic goals for their marriage and their two young children.

4. They attend a Bible-preaching church and are growing week by week.

5. They have many close Christian friends.

6. God's Holy Spirit leads and guides them daily.

7. They have similar ambitions.

Are they without problems? No, but their problems and disappointments are minor ones that are relatively easy to handle and overcome. Do they ever have illness or do they experience disappointments? Yes, but Christ is their source of strength.

In short, this couple has the strongest glue known to mankind to cement a marriage and make it successful: *spirituality!*

God, who instituted marriage and the family, wants to be the center of every marriage. He tells Christians not to be unequally yoked with unbelievers. Then he offers guidance every day.

But many people do not have this spiritual glue to cement their marriage. They aren't doing well . . . and they probably never will, until they surrender their lives to Christ and live for Him unreservedly.

Marriage cannot function well without the Lord. Since people are spiritual beings created by God, and have a capacity for experiencing God, they must be spiritually fulfilled if they are to live effective, happy lives.

Problems of marriage are on the minds of millions. Their lives are unhappy and unfulfilling. Because my daily radio broadcast, Psychology For Living, has been aired widely for many years, I receive large volumes of mail. Much of it is from husbands and wives who are dissatisfied with their marriage—especially wives.[1]

Perhaps the most common problem that comes to our attention persistently is that in which one partner is saved and the other is not.[2] Here is "Janet," for example. Some years ago she married "Jim." But after several months of marriage it became quite plain to her that he did not know Christ as his personal Savior. Time went on and several children came into this unequally yoked family. Naturally, Janet was never encouraged by her husband to live for the Lord. So she never developed adequately in her spiritual life.

Through the years Janet has received a little spiritual encouragement. For two years she had a neighbor who loved the Lord Jesus Christ, and this neighbor encouraged Janet. At another time she attended a Sunday-school class taught by a man and his wife who took time to visit Janet and inspired her in her spiritual walk. But for the most part Janet has not grown spiritually. Consequently, life is quite discouraging for her.

Janet has not been able to teach her children about the Lord because her unsaved husband criticized her at every point. True, she smuggled in a little Bible teaching. But it was sparse and spasmodic. Two of the children have shown some interest in spiritual matters, but the other two have not.

Another serious problem in Janet's and Jim's home is the fact that he cannot offer leadership. Since he is unsaved, he is going in one direction and Janet in another. Consequently, "leadership" is virtually impossible. The Bible clearly teaches that the husband has a definite responsibility for spiritual leadership of the family. But if he does not know the Lord, he cannot adequately lead them.

"But the natural man receiveth not the things of the Spirit of

God: for they are foolishness unto him: neither can he know them, because they are spiritually discerned" (1 Corinthians 2:14).

Jim and Janet aren't even together, much less leading and following. Jim's unsaved condition brings about many other problems. For example, Janet would like to see their children attend Christian schools and eventually enroll in a Christian college. But Jim will have none of this. "Why spend money for that school when they can attend a public school?" he asks. So the children are being taught in secular schools where there is little respect for God or the Bible.

This divided home has another serious problem—a social one. Janet would like to go to activities at church, and take the children places that honor Christ. But Jim is not interested. They can't agree on friends. Jim is not interested in Janet's "religious" friends. And Janet can't put up with Jim's drinking, "ungodly" crowd.

This turmoil prevents Janet and Jim from getting along well. They have many disagreements, quarrels, and heartaches. Intimate relationships also suffer. It's almost impossible for them to have good love relationships when they are going in opposite directions, living in opposite worlds, and disagreeing on almost everything. Sex has lost its luster.

Unfortunately, the world is filled with such couples. One is saved, but not doing well. The other is unsaved and unhappy. Naturally, they are not able to meet the basic emotional needs of their children. Consequently, their sons and daughters grow up with emotional deprivation. By the time the children are grown, these frustrations, hostilities and insecurities will be a definite part of their personalities. They will be handicapped as long as they live, unless they get some special help.

Can anything be done for a couple like this?

Yes, but it isn't easy. The wife must make a number of changes, and so must the husband. The wife should understand that since she is the one who knows Christ personally, she must make the first move. She must be as kind and understanding as she can be to her husband, realizing that he does not have the Holy Spirit within him to guide and change him. She should spend time with her husband, encouraging him at every point. She must not abandon her own beliefs and Christian contacts to join his unsaved friends and beliefs. She must spend much time in prayer and reading God's Word so that she can be strong and be used by God to help him. She should take every opportunity that seems wise to encourage him to go where he can experience a Christian influence and be saved. She must realize, too, that her husband is just as precious in God's sight as she is, and that *He wants to save him.*

A year or so ago I met a couple like Jim and Janet. What problems they had! But recently he gave his life to Christ. Now he is reading God's Word, and praying and fellowshipping with believers. His spiritual growth is phenomenal. His new life is making a real difference in their marriage.

One lady writing me from Canada recently said, "I told you three years ago about my unsaved husband and the fact that our marriage was disintegrating. Well, six months ago he came to know Christ as his Savior and he is growing tremendously. We have fallen in love all over again and we have never been so happy as we are now."

What happened to this unequally yoked couple can happen to you, or anyone who has a problem. Nothing is more important than a life in Christ, to bring two people together and hold them securely and happily!

Up to this point we have discussed some of the spiritual aspects of marriage. But now I'd like to turn our attention to personality problems.

Whether you are saved or lost, you may have personality hangups that are preventing you from having a successful marriage. If you studied 1,000 couples who are unhappy in their marriage, you would find that the great majority are marked by personality maladjustments either on the part of the wife, the husband, or both.

Take the "Smiths" for example. After quarreling and bickering for years, they finally went to see a psychologist. During their second session of counseling, both were given psychological tests. The initial sessions plus the testing pointed up, among other things, that Mrs. Smith was very insecure. Mr. Smith's test showed that his personality was marked by a great deal of hostility. These traits were not little, insignificant, temporary attitudes. Instead they were deep, persistent traits that showed themselves in nearly everything the Smiths said and did. They were showing up all day, every day. Nor had these traits come about recently. They had been there a long time. Their roots extended back through the early years of their childhood.

As we study human beings and their development in the early

years of life, we realize that they have basic emotional needs that cry out for fulfillment. This is the way God has made human beings. As a child grows up, for example, he needs to feel (among other things) that he *belongs*. He needs thousands of experiences during each year of his early life that tell him loudly and clearly that he *does* belong. These signals of belongingness are given primarily by the mother and the father. If this belongingness material is fed into the computer of his life, he will grow up with healthy feelings about himself. Without actually realizing it, he knows that he does belong. By the time he is grown, this feeling is instilled deeply into his life, and it serves him well throughout his lifetime.

This is true of all of the basic emotional needs, not just the need of belonging.[3]

Many parents are not aware of children's basic emotional needs, much less prepared to meet them! As a result, a child's needs may never be met.

There are many passive ways of failing to meet a child's basic emotional needs. For example, the father can be busy with his work, never spending much time with his child. The child is overlooked. He doesn't feel that he belongs or that he is loved. On the other hand, parents can take very aggressive measures that add up to not meeting basic emotional needs. For example, a mother may scream and yell at a child day by day for years. By this continual behavior, she is telling the child that he does not belong. And so the list goes—hundreds and hundreds of things that parents can do and *not* do, failing to meet the basic emotional needs of their children.

In time these children grow up, and these personality traits are deep within them. And they tend to remain there and help to control the person's thoughts and actions and responses for a lifetime.

Interestingly enough, most adults are not aware of how they act, and how their behavior may be a long distance from center. In other words, a person may feel quite hostile and yet never know that he is hostile. The way he feels seems to be normal for him. As a woman told me once, she just "felt the way she felt." And during a person's life he tends to adjust to his personality maladjustments. He works around them. But they are producing a negative effect upon his life and, of course, his mate.

In marriage these personality hangups become like thorns.

They prick people the wrong way. They prevent a person from having the dynamic relationships that he could have with other people, and with his Lord.

Is there any hope for marriage partners who have personality hangups? Yes, indeed! But change always begins with insight. Until a person is aware that he is hostile, or paranoid, or insecure, or withdrawn, he probably will never change. The Bible usually does not affect a person's behavior unless he is aware that he does have a problem, and that he needs to seek Biblical guidance.

Through professional counseling with a godly therapist, a person can become aware of his personality maladjustments and change them. This, then, will lead to a much happier and fulfilling life!

---

[1]See also *God's Will in Your Marriage* by Clyde M. Narramore. A free copy is available from the Narramore Christian Foundation, Rosemead, California, 91770.

[2]See also *Married to an Unbeliever,* Narramore Christian Foundation.

[3]See also Clyde M. Narramore, *This Way to Happiness* (Grand Rapids, Michigan: Zondervan).

THE CHURCH

The Unchurched American

by George Gallup, Jr.

Introduction

Some 61 million American adults are not members of any church or religious institution. Moreover, some churches are experiencing a continuing decline in membership.

What can churches do to encourage the "unchurched"—many of whom are strong believers—to become part of the community of active worshippers?

There are, of course, no easy answers. Habits and attitudes cannot be changed overnight. For example, eight in ten Americans believe that one can be a good Christian or Jew and not attend church or synagogue.

This study is the first to deal specifically with the values, interests, and backgrounds of the unchurched. It covers a wide range of factors related to churchlessness, including beliefs, lifestyles, upbringing, training, and social/inter personal relations. Are people unchurched by choice or do they feel excluded? Are some people just "unreachable"?

Through use of the control group method, the survey provides an in-depth profile of what unchurched Americans are like and how they compare with persons who are affiliated with churches.

The results of the study provide a practical guide for the clergy in reaching the unchurched. The study seeks to answer three central questions:

1. Who are the "unchurched" and how do they differ from the "churched"?
2. What factors lead to becoming unchurched?
3. What can churches do to encourage the unchurched to become part of the community of active worshipers?

The study provides an up-to-date examination of America's religious climate as a backdrop for comparing the churched and the unchurched. Key questions about basic religious beliefs and practices have been repeated from surveys conducted in 1952 and 1965, and reveal changes that have occurred over the last quarter century (the 1952 survey was conducted for the Catholic Digest by Ben Gaffin Associates; the 1965 survey was conducted for the Catholic Digest by the Gallup Organization, Inc.).

Definition of "Unchurched"

For the purpose of this study, the working definition of the "unchurched" is a person who is not a member of a church or synagogue or who has not attended church or synagogue in the last six months, apart from weddings, funerals, or special holidays such as Christmas, Easter, or Yom Kippur. Persons who are unchurched, while not meeting the criteria for the "churched" in this study, may of course include in their number deeply religious persons who do not happen to be drawn to the institutional church—or who, for some valid reason such as health problems, are unable to attend church regularly.

Using the above definition, 41 percent of all adults in the current study can be classified as "unchurched" while 59 percent can be classified as "churched" (that is, have attended church or synagogue other than on a holiday and are members of a church).

The 41 percent who are classified as unchurched projects to approximately 61 million adults (18 years and older), while the 59 percent churched projects to approximately 89 million adults. These projections are based on the U.S. Department of Labor's April 1978 estimate of the total adult civilian non-institutionalized population. This estimate was 150,116,000.

Factors Examined in This Study

Many factors are related to churchgoing and non-churchgoing. The following is a list of some of the key factors examined in this study:

—Basic religious beliefs; theological and philosophical factors.
—Religious practice and participation (including prayer, churchgoing, Bible reading, meditation).
—Self-assessment in terms of religious beliefs.
—Attitudes toward the institutional church.
—Values and goals in life.
—Outlook on life.
—Lifestyle patterns.
—Demographic and lifecycle factors.
—Involvement in organizations; interests.
—Attitudes toward key institutions in society.
—Influence of family and home environment.
—Interpersonal relations; social status.
—Mobility.
—Travel.
—Activities on Sunday.
—Impact of radio and television.

Major Points

The study deals with four major areas: general attitudes; attitudes toward organized religion; religious commitment; and religious background. Among the major findings that emerge from the study are the following:

I. *General Attitudes*

A. The results of this survey show nationwide acceptance of traditional values. While the 1960's and 1970's have sometimes been labeled decades of revolt and disillusionment, the 1980's may come to be regarded as a period of "return to normalcy."

Comparison of the churched and unchurched shows that large majorities of both groups would welcome "more emphasis on traditional family ties," and "more respect for authority."

Both groups would also welcome "more emphasis on working hard," although a slightly higher proportion of the churched than the unchurched would do so.

Results for the total sample (including both churched and unchurched) show the following:

- Nine in 10 (89 percent) say they would welcome more respect for authority in the coming years;
- A similar proportion (91 percent) would welcome more emphasis on traditional family ties;

- Seven in 10 (69 percent) say they would welcome more emphasis on working hard;
- Three out of every four (74 percent) would not like to see more acceptance of marijuana usage; and
- Six in 10 (62 percent) would be opposed to more acceptance of sexual freedom.

While Americans (both the churched and unchurched) appear to be strongly traditionalist in certain key respects, they depart somewhat from widely accepted views in terms of other questions. For example:

- Seven out of every 10 (70 percent) would welcome less emphasis on money;
- Three in four (75 percent) say they would welcome more emphasis on self-expression.

Younger adults (18 to 29 years old) and those with a college background tend to be more liberal in their outlook regarding social changes, particularly those related to morals. However, differences in terms of age groups and education level are not so marked as might be expected.

The study shows, for example, that an overwhelming majority of young people (both the churched and unchurched) say they would welcome more emphasis on family ties and more respect for authority.

The sharpest differences between younger and older Americans are found in regard to acceptance of marijuana usage and sexual freedom. Young people are much more likely than are their elders to say they would welcome both more acceptance of marijuana usage and sexual freedom.

B. In terms of values, the views of the churched and the unchurched differ most sharply on matters of personal freedom.

While a minority in both groups say they would welcome greater acceptance of sexual freedom and of marijuana usage, the unchurched are far more likely to welcome such changes.

In addition, the study also found that of 22 statements about churches, the churched and unchurched disagree most about the statement, "the rules about morality preached by the churches and synagogues today are too restrictive."

Furthermore, among those who are unchurched 53 percent feel it is "always wrong" to have extramarital sex, while among the churched, the figure is 74 percent.

Among those with a high-school background or a grade-school

background, the percentages who say extramarital sex is "always wrong" are 66 and 80 percent, respectively.

Differences between men and women are not so marked although women are slightly more likely to say "always wrong." Protestants (71 percent) are somewhat more likely to hold this view than are Catholics (64 percent).

II. *Attitudes Toward Organized Religion*

A. Public confidence in the church or organized religion is higher than it is in eight other key institutions of society. About six in ten nationally express a "great deal" or "quite a lot" of confidence in the church or organized religion.

When churched and unchurched views are compared, the differences are dramatic: Eighty percent of churched people express a "great deal" or "quite a lot" of confidence in the church, but only 38 percent of the unchurched do so.

In the case of the eight other institutions tested, little difference is found between the views of the churched and unchurched.

B. Organized religion is widely criticized by the unchurched as having lost "the real spiritual part of religion" and for being "too concerned with organizational as opposed to theological or spiritual issues."

Large majorities of the unchurched agree (strongly or moderately) with these statements. They believe that "most churches are not effective in helping people find meaning in life" and fail to be "concerned enough with social justice."

Significantly, these criticisms are shared by large proportions of the churched, as well.

- Six in ten among the unchurched, and as many as half of the churched, agree (strongly or moderately) with the statement, "most churches and synagogues have lost the real spiritual part of religion."
- Fifty-six percent of the unchurched say "most churches and synagogues today are too concerned with organizational as opposed to theological or spiritual issues," and 47 percent of the churched agree.
- Forty-nine percent of the unchurched, and 39 percent of the churched, agree with the statement "most churches and synagogues today are not concerned enough with social justice."

Significant and comparable proportions of both unchurched (36 percent) and churched (28 percent) are critical of churches and synagogues as "not warm and accepting outsiders."

Perhaps most telling of all is the finding that 86 percent of the unchurched—and 76 percent of the churched—agree that "an individual should arrive at his or her own religious beliefs independent of any churches or synagogues."

The churched and unchurched are in close agreement that "commitment to a meaningful career is very important" and that "depending on how much strength and character a person has he can pretty well control what happens to him."

The churched, however, are much more likely than are the unchurched to say they have "discovered clear-cut goals and a satisfying life purpose" and to say "facing my daily tasks is a source of pleasure and satisfaction."

Can a person be a good Christian or Jew if he or she doesn't attend church or synagogue? Seven out of ten of the churched segment, and eight persons in ten of the unchurched, answer in the affirmative.

C. While there has been little decline in the proportion of Americans who hold to basic beliefs, a smaller proportion of people today than in 1965 and in 1952 say religion plays a key role in their lives. About half (53 percent) of the current sample say religion is "very important" in their lives; the comparable percentages were 70 percent in 1965 and 75 percent in 1952.

Among the churched, 70 percent say religion is "very important" in their lives, while proportion is considerably lower, 30 percent, among the unchurched.

III. *Religious Commitment*

A. The proportion of *believers* has remained constant over the last quarter century.

Today, as in 1965 and 1952, about eight Americans in ten believe that Jesus Christ is God or the Son of God. Thirteen percent in the current survey believe Jesus was "another leader like Muhammad," almost exactly matching the proportions recorded in the earlier surveys. As in the earlier surveys, one percent believe Jesus never actually existed.

In belief in life after death, little change has occurred, as determined by comparable questions asked over the last quarter century. Today, as earlier, about seven in ten say they believe in life after death.

The proportion who say they pray to God is currently about nine in ten, the same proportion as recorded in 1965 and 1952. A decline in frequency of prayer, however, is noted.

B. The unchurched are overwhelmingly "believers" and it is not a loss of faith, in most cases, that has caused people to become unchurched.

Sociologist Dean Hoge of the Catholic University of America notes: "The proportion of Americans who are unchurched for philosophical reasons is not great. Other forces seem to be more determinative, such as interpersonal influences, community relationships and life styles."

The unchurched, as defined in this study, appear to be remarkably religious in certain basic respects, that is, many say they believe in the resurrection of Jesus Christ and a relatively high proportion claim a religious or "born again" experience.

A total of 93 percent of the churched and 68 percent of the unchurched say they believe in the resurrection of Jesus Christ.

Nine in ten (89 percent) of the churched and 64 percent of the unchurched believe that Jesus is God or the Son of God. Six percent of the churched group believe Jesus was another religious leader like Muhammad or Buddha, while 21 percent of the unchurched hold this view. Fewer than one percent of the churched (two percent of the unchurched) think Jesus Christ never actually existed.

Four out of five churched say they have made a commitment to Jesus Christ, compared to two in five among the unchurched.

More than eight in ten (83 percent) of the churched and six in ten (57 percent) of the unchurched believe in a life after death.

The churched are about equally divided between those who believe the Bible to be the "actual word of God" and those who believe it is the "inspired word of God." Three percent of the churched, but 20 percent of the unchurched, believe the Bible to be an "ancient book of fables."

When asked if they "ever pray to God," 98 percent of the churched group reply in the affirmative, but 76 percent of the unchurched do so as well.

Of the total sample of churched, 74 percent indicate that they pray frequently (that is, once a day or more), while 45 percent of the unchurched do so.

Nearly as high a proportion of the churches (seven percent) as the unchurched (ten percent) practice a specific technique of meditation—such as those taught in Transcendental Meditation, Zen, Divine Light Mission, and the like.

About four in ten of the churched group (43 percent) say they have had a religious experience—that is, a particularly powerful religious insight awakening—compared to 24 percent of the unchurched.

IV. *Religious Background*

A. Most of the presently unchurched have had a traditionally religious background—in fact, to about the same extent as the churched.

About nine in ten (88 percent) among the churched have received religious training of some sort as a child, compared to 77 percent of the unchurched.

The sharpest difference found between the churched and unchurched in terms of the kind of training is "instruction by your parents at home," cited by the churched considerably more often than by the unchurched.

Those comprising the churched segment are far more likely than the unchurched to say they have received some religious education as an adult, other than during a worship service, within the last two years.

As for preparation for confirmation or for full membership in the church or synagogue, 54 percent of the churched say they have had such training, in contrast to 40 percent among the unchurched.

An overwhelming majority of those in the "churched" category (95 percent) would want a child of theirs to receive religious instruction. However, as many as 74 percent of the unchurched give the same response.

In addition, the churched are more likely to say their children are currently receiving religious training—72 percent do so compared to 43 percent among the unchurched.

In terms of the total sample, a decline is found in the percentage of Americans who say they have received religious training as a child, from 94 percent in 1952 to 91 percent in 1965 to 83 percent today.

It is interesting to note that this downtrend (in religious training) parallels a downtrend in the percentage of Americans who say religion is "very important" in their lives.

B. The basic reason why the churched joined the church or

synagogue was because they were brought up in the congregation. Nearly half of the responses fall into this category.

Friends, good preaching, and a good program of religious education are also cited as reasons for choosing a particular church.

Significantly, one of the reasons given is "I was invited to this church by a member, and I liked the people."

C. Factors that led returnees (churched, unchurched, and rechurched) to resume attending include (1) self need; (2) so that children could have religious instruction; (3) a matter of faith; and (4) a personal religious experience.

D. A significant proportion (one in four) of the presently churched indicate there was a period of two years or more when they were among the unchurched—that is, did not attend church or synagogue.

Those survey respondents (both churched and unchurched) who indicated there was a period of two years or more when they did not attend church or synagogue were asked for reasons for not doing so. The churched group are most likely to say "I moved to a different community and never got involved in a new church" or "I found other interests and activities, which led me to spend less and less time on church-related activities."

The unchurched, on the other hand, are most likely to say "when I grew up and started making decisions on my own, I stopped going to church."

E. Many interests compete with churchgoing among those who have never become reaffiliated with a church or synagogue. They were, "sports, recreational activity, and hobbies," "social activities with friends," "a work schedule that made it difficult to attend church," and "the desire for more time for myself and/or family."

F. When those who have moved to a new community were asked why they never became reaffiliated with a new church or synagogue, the chief reason given (by 42 percent) is that "seeking a new church was not a matter of urgency and I never got around to it."

The reason cited next most frequently (by 14 percent) is "none of the churches near my home was to my liking." Next (by ten percent) is "there were no churches of my preferred denomination at a convenient distance from my new home."

G. When the unchurched are asked to indicate the reasons they became less involved with the church, a complex of reasons is offered. These range from problems that the church might be able to overcome to problems over which the church has little control, such as one's work schedule or illness.

Frequently cited are: competing activities, objections to the church (its teaching or members), making decisions on one's own, moving to a different community, the belief that the church was no longer helping in the search for meaning or purpose in life, and a different lifestyle.

H. Those who say they had problems with the church (which contributed to their reduced involvement) were asked about specific problems. Cited most often, 37 percent, is that "the teachings about beliefs were too narrow." Next are "the moral teachings were too narrow" and "a dislike for the traditional forms of worship" (28 percent).

Of particular significance is the finding that about one individual in five is critical of the church because "I wanted deeper spiritual meaning than I found in the church or synagogue."

Interestingly, attitudes on the church's involvement in social and political issues cut both ways: One person in six expressed the feeling that "the church or synagogue isn't willing to change society," while about an equal proportion claimed "a dislike for church or synagogue involvement in social or political issues."

I. Many of the unchurched—while not drawn to organized religion—nevertheless have positive inclinations toward organized religion and feel that "religion is a good thing." For example, the overwhelming majority of the unchurched would like to have their children receive religious training.

J. At least half of the unchurched (52 percent or approximately 20 million adults) say they could see a situation where they could become a "fairly active member of a church now" and would be open to an invitation from the church community.

K. Differences between the churched and the unchurched also include the following:

- Those who are churched are more likely than are the unchurched to have all or most of their closest friends living in the same community. And they are four times more likely to say that all or most of their closest friends attend a church or synagogue on a regular basis.
- Churched people are more likely to be "joiners." Thirty-eight percent of this group belong to one or more voluntary organizations in their communities other than a church or religious

group, compared to 25 percent among the unchurched segment.

- The churched have lived longer in the same community than the unchurched: 26 percent have lived in their communities five years or less, while 38 percent of the unchurched fall into this category.
  Furthermore, 18 percent of the churched have moved two or more times, but 30 percent of the unchurched have done so.
- They are more likely to be men than women, young than old, single than married. Level of formal education does not appear to be a major factor. Nor are sharp differences found between Protestants and Catholics.

Commentary

The job of encouraging and persuading the unchurched to become part of the community of active worshippers will not be an easy one. Clearly, organized religion is not playing a central role in the religious lives of a sizable proportion of the unchurched. Many feel they can "go it alone."

In addition, many outside the church—and inside as well—are critical of churches. Organized religion is widely criticized by the unchurched as having lost the "real spiritual part of religion" and for being "too concerned with organizational as opposed to theological or spiritual issues." Large majorities of the unchurched also believe that "most churches are not effective in helping people find meaning to life."

Furthermore, we appear to be in a period of what has been described as "secular drift." Religion has lost some of its importance in our lives when the data from the current study are compared with data from the 1965 and 1952 surveys.

While there has been no collapse in faith in the U.S. over the last quarter century, the nature or direction of our beliefs appears to have changed somewhat. David Roozen, Coordinator of Research at the Hartford Seminary Foundation, suggests that a comparison of survey findings from the current study with those from the studies in 1965 and 1952 indicates a "gradual shift from literal fundamentalist interpretations of traditional Christian doctrines to symbolic/liberal interpretations."

Peggy Shriver, Assistant General Secretary of the Office of Research Evaluation and Planning of the National Council of the Churches of Christ, in commenting on the results of the Unchurched American study for *The Yearbook of American and Canadian Churches, 1979,* succinctly summarizes some of the major challenges facing churches today:

> The task of church renewal appears formidable. Beliefs without strong conviction, a faith that seems to require no corporate expression, some persons seeking more vital spiritual depth, many others insisting on more latitude in moral teachings and beliefs—these are familiar stones in the American mosaic. In prayerful response the church must continue to be the church of Jesus Christ.

In addition to the basic factors underlying churchlessness, various practical matters also keep people from becoming involved. These are detailed in other parts of this report.

Bringing unchurched Americans to a realization of the spiritual rewards of being part of the community of active believers will be a difficult task. Yet some of the findings from the study justify optimism. The Reverend Alvin A. Illig, C.S.P., Executive Director, National Conference of Catholic Bishops Ad Hoc Committee on Evangelism had this to say:

> I am greatly encouraged that the programs of outreach we will be designing as a result of this study will in God's good time be beneficial:
> —52 percent of the unchurched Americans see a situation where they could become active members of a church today!
> —23 percent of the 91 million churchgoing adults had a period of two years or more when they were among the unchurched. This says to me that with tactful effort, with sensitivity, with patient listening and understanding, with genuine love, and with the power of the Holy Spirit, many, many millions of the 61 million unchurched Americans will 'come back home.'
> —Almost four out of five of the unchurched want their children to have some religious education. Obviously, there is a tremendous reservoir of good will with which we have to work.
> —Some two-thirds of the unchurched today pray, believe in God, believe in Jesus Christ as the Son of God, believe in an afterlife. We are dealing with a people who have deep religious roots, roots that when watered with kindness and compassion will once more grow.

Perhaps the most significant finding for me as an ordained priest with many years of theological study behind me is that the reasons why people return to church participation most often are not the profound theological questions we debated in the seminary—important though they are—questions which are extremely difficult to understand and extremely difficult to convey. Most of the reasons for leaving as well as most of the reasons for returning deal with human factors, factors which are often manageable if we are but sensitive to the bruises, the needs, the yearnings, the inadequacies of the churchless. When meditated upon, the Gallup Study of the Unchurched could be a very humanizing influence on priests, ministers and rabbis who at times, both consciously and unconsciously, alienate people through our own inhumanity.

Possible Steps to Help Bring About Renewal

1. *Reevaluate your program of religious education.* To the extent one is able to judge an institution by its product, one could ask certain questions about programs of religious education. Survey evidence indicates that many adult Americans—including those with a Sunday-school background—have a shocking lack of knowledge about the Bible and key facts of their religion.

Sunday-school and CCD classes have been called by some "the most wasted hour of the week." Whether or not this is true is a question for debate. The fact remains that nearly as high a proportion of the unchurched as the churched say they have attended Sunday school.

Perhaps it would be appropriate to reexamine and reevaluate your program of religious education. Are children learning the basic facts about their religion? Is the program enriching their religious and spiritual lives? Is the curriculum suited for each particular age level?

Are teachers of Christianity not only dealing with information about Christ but also with the formation of His character in today's youth? Are children putting their beliefs into actual life situations? Is belief followed by commitment? Is Christianity presented not only as a creed but also as a relationship with a living Christ? Is the teacher a dedicated and inspired Christian or Jew—or simply the only person available?

2. *Strengthen your program of spiritual counseling.* Among those who could be brought back to the church, most cite as an important motivation, "If I can find a pastor with whom I can openly discuss my religious doubts and my spiritual needs."

By way of background, it is worth noting that Western religions are sometimes criticized as having neglected the role of spiritual counseling so prominent in Eastern religions.

Others among the unchurched complain that churches have not

helped them find "meaning in their lives." Here, too, spiritual counseling could help.

3. *Reexamine the status of religion in the home.* One of the greatest differences between the churched and unchurched found in the study is that the former are more likely to have had religious training in the home.

Many religious leaders maintain that the home, not the church, should be the center of Christian or Jewish education. Yet the facts clearly indicate that many parents—churched as well as the unchurched—are not doing their job.

It clearly behooves the clergy and others involved in religious education to gain insight into the conditions in the home in terms of religious training. Does the family talk about God and religion? Is the Bible read regularly? Does the family pray together? What is the nature of devotions in the home? Are efforts made to apply the gospel precepts to the formation of character in the home?

What do parents themselves know about their faith? Do they practice their faith? How do they deal with the tough questions asked by their offspring? How many parents, particularly if they themselves do not go to church, can give a good answer to the child's question: "Why should I go to church?"

What is called for is a "team effort" between clergy and parents—to find out how churches can complement and reinforce what is taught in the home, to educate parents, to educate youngsters and to aid in their spiritual upbringing.

Such efforts are likely to be welcomed by parents, since both the churched and unchurched say they would like to have their children receive religious training.

Furthermore, this clergy-parent team effort would enrich the spiritual lives of families, improve relationships among family members and thereby help combat the trend toward the dissolution of the family unit. In addition, such efforts would likely help reduce the problem of discipline in our schools—which has consistently been named the number one problem in annual Kettering-Gallup surveys on education.

4. *Develop an active program of evangelism.* Clergymen should perhaps do more to encourage church members to feel that evangelism and witnessing are key aspects of religious commitment.

The study indicates that while much evangelism is being undertaken—particularly by members of the more evangelical churches—a great deal more could be done. Indeed, one of the key reasons given by those who joined a church is that someone invited them to do so.

In each community of worshipers, certain people are particularly effective in reaching others. The style of evangelism should be adapted to the particular situation. In some cases, a "hard sell" may repel rather than attract prospective church members. Evangelism can also be understood in terms of a counseling relationship with those who wish to mature in Christ.

Evangelism often fails, not only because the evangelizer occasionally "comes on too strong," but because he or she does not address the particular needs of a given person, whether material needs or spiritual. In this respect, churches would do well to experiment with different approaches to see which are most effective.

> —Deal with the problems of life. Surveys have frequently shown that religiously involved people are often more able to cope with life's many problems than are those who are not religiously involved.
> —Strengthen the religious and moral development of their children. Most parents put a high premium on the religious development of their children.
> —Understand the meaning of life. Many people today—in what has been called the "Me Decade"—appear to be searching for a deeper dimension to their lives.
> —Enrich their own spiritual lives. Many of the unchurched have active spiritual lives and pray regularly. Those involved in evangelization could point out how this prayer life could be nourished in a church context, through prayer meetings, discussion groups and the like.

Many of the unchurched—and churched as well—feel that churches are "spiritually dry." Americans—particularly the young—are increasingly turning to various religious movements and disciplines in an effort to find deeper spiritual meaning in their lives. A significant proportion of Americans have had a dramatic religious experience in their lives but are spiritually homeless—they are all charged up, but feel they have no place to go.

Churches need to be more open to an understanding or religious experience and to help people build upon these periods or moments of religious insight or awakening.

Some clergymen appear puzzled and perhaps distrustful of such open expressions of piety. Yet an increasing number of churches—mainline as well as evangelical—are instituting programs such as "spiritual journeys" in which people describe their own religious struggles. The impact on listeners can often be profound.

5. *Reach out to new people in a community.* Sometimes all that people need is an invitation. The study indicates that many people have never been asked to try a new church, but would do so if they received an invitation.

The potential for new members may be more encouraging than in the past, since many people apparently are spiritually restless. In addition, denominational lines are not as strong as they have been in the past. Perhaps church leaders could explore the possibility of extending the outreach of their churches to include "home services" or "house churches" for those living a considerable distance from church.

6. *Build on—rather than compete with—religious broadcasting.* An increasing number of Americans get their religion through the broadcast media. Rather than compete with this growing trend, churches might do well to make greater use of radio and television.

Church programs could be designed to supplement and complement religious TV and radio broadcasts, with follow-up discussions and commentary. Pastors could themselves become involved in religious broadcasting.

Such efforts would certainly seem worthwhile since most Americans are avid television viewers and since a significant proportion of the unchurched are reached in this fashion.

7. *Examine and evaluate the effectiveness of your mission.* Are you getting through to your congregation? What are the levels of religious practice, belief and knowledge? Surveys can show you how the results of your own church or synagogue compare with regional and national norms. The Princeton Religion Research Center is in the process of writing a church survey manual for use by local churches.

What about the future?
While the challenges facing the churches of America in their efforts to reach the unchurched are immense, the study offers reason to be encouraged. Donald W. Kimmick, Rector of the

Church of the Good Shepherd in Midland Park, New Jersey, sums up the message of the study on the Unchurched American in these words:

> Look at this recent Gallup survey! I am a parish pastor and a social researcher and the results show me great opportunity for the church.
> Of the 61 million Americans who are not members of a church, 52 percent say they might see themselves becoming fairly active members now. What would bring these people into the Body of Christ?
> —A church that would listen to religious doubts and spiritual need.
> —A church with vital worship and preaching.
> —A church with a real thirst for Christian education at its best.
> —A church that will simply invite them to join.
>
> May God help us to achieve these worthwhile goals.

If efforts to reach out to the unchurched meet with success, what will this mean for the churches of the U.S.?

Predictions are risky, of course, but the fact may be that the unchurched—many of whom are deeply religious and perhaps in some ways more creative in their spiritual lives—could, if brought back into the community of active worshipers, do as much to revitalize the churches of our nation as the churched themselves.

What Price Evangelism?

by Dr. Harold Lindsell

Evangelism is in trouble today. This is true even though large numbers of people are being won to Christ among the less educated peoples of Africa and Latin America. In the western world, however, scholars are undercutting evangelism as the churches have known it in past generations. Moreover, not nearly as many people in the west are coming to Christ as they are in other parts of the globe. This brings to the fore the question: What *is* happening among the scholars, the intelligentsia, and the leadership of the churches with respect to evangelism?

The Biblical Basis for Evangelism

Traditionally it is accurate to say that the Christian faith has been long regarded as unique, that is, generically different from all the other religions in the world. It was not looked upon as one religion among many, but as the only true religion outside of which salvation was not possible. It was accepted as God's divinely ordained vehicle through which the gospel was brought to men. Even among the neoorthodox, such as Karl Barth, the absolute uniqueness of Christianity was affirmed. Hendrick Kraemer in his book *The Christian Message in the Non-Christian World* said the same thing.

Since Jesus Christ is the central personage in the Christian faith, He has also been looked upon as the only Savior of men. Peter affirmed that "there is none other name under heaven given among men, whereby we must be saved" (Acts 4:12). This is the finality, the uniqueness, and the only saviorhood of Jesus expressed, for example, by Robert E. Speer, the great missionary statesman, and the Edinburgh Missionary conclave in 1910 despite a few dissenting voices.

Today the historic Biblical foundation on which evangelism has been based is being questioned, denied, and watered down. The study of comparative religions has come into its full flower and is responsible for this. It is undergirded by humanistic presuppositions which deny the final and full authority of the Bible. Thus scholars in this field grade religions like candlers grade eggs. Whatever the size or the color, an egg is an egg. Whatever the differences between Christianity and other faiths, they are all said to be legitimate alternatives and true bearers of salvation.

Carl E. Braaten, professor of systematic theology at the Lutheran School of Theology at Chicago, wrote an article which appeared in the January 1980 missionary *Occasional Bulletin*. In that article he repudiated the notion of Christianity's exclusiveness, and took serious issue with the Lausanne Covenant, which said all men outside of Christ are forever lost. He agreed with and supported the statement, "The teaching that there is salvation in the other religions is spreading in the churches." "The reason Christians are confused and have appeared so smug about salvation," he said, "is that they imagined they had a monopoly on salvation." He went on to attempt a reconciliation of opposing viewpoints only to end up with a universalism related to the person of Jesus in which all men are saved at last. He wrote: "The ultimate horizon of this historically mediated universality is hope for an eternal restitution of all things in God." This approach emasculates and destroys what Christians have affirmed through the ages. And it leads to the tougher question why Christians ought to spend time, money, and effort to convert the unbelieving since all things will be restored at last.

Universalism, that is, the ultimate salvation of all men and all things, has become a fixed part of the theological pattern of the World Council of Churches. This agency has been deeply influenced and affected by this viewpoint. As a consequence, the council has expressed little or no concern for evangelism .and missionary outreach designed to bring the gospel to those who have never heard. Since all will be redeemed, the mission of the church has been reduced to social, economic, and political action. Changing the structures of society, improving the temporal condition of men's lives, and bringing in socialism under a commitment to the Marxist view of history constitute the most important items on the agenda of the World Council of Churches.

Syncretism is one of the common strands woven into the skein of universalism. Once universalism is accepted, salvation of necessity can be found in all the other religions. When this step is taken, truth is found in the non-Christian faiths, and no reason can be advanced why whatever is "good" in any other religion should not be incorporated into the Christian faith. Nor is there any reason not to remove from the Christian faith anything thought to be "bad." Even if one does not accept the basic components found in any of the other religions, it is possible to adopt the view of the former Dean of the Yale Divinity School, Colin Williams, who was quoted in *Christianity Today* years ago as saying: "I'm not afraid of a plurality of truth. This doesn't mean that I don't make distinctions, but only that I hold it open that what is true for the Buddhist in his situation may be as valid for him as mine is for me."

Syncretism, universalism, and salvation within the other religions are surpassed in their dangers by the recent and alarming rise of the denial that Jesus Christ is God. The attack on the deity of Jesus and thus on the doctrine of the Trinity is not new, but there has been a dramatic resurgence of that attack. John Hick's recent book, which expressed the views of five other scholars as well as his own, was a concerted attack on Christ's deity. It was powerfully answered by John R. W. Stott in *Christianity Today*. John Hick was rewarded for his book by an appointment to the faculty of the Claremont Graduate School in California. In the January 20, 1980, *Los Angeles Times* he was reported as saying, "The calling of any faith the only true religion is a form of bigotry. God as experienced by this or that individual is real, not illusory, and yet the experience of God is partial and is adapted to our human spiritual capacities. If this thesis is accepted then the very plurality and variety of the human experience of God provides a wider basis for theology than can the experience of any one religious tradition taken by itself."

Once the deity of Jesus Christ is rejected, the atonement is nullified, the doctrine of the Trinity becomes passe, and the question left open why anyone should take the Great Commission seriously when the foundations of the faith have been so thoroughly discredited. What is significant about all of this is that the proponents who emasculate the Christian faith are not atheists, agnostics, or adherents of the non-Christian religions. The opposition comes from within the church by those who at least in theory profess to be Christians. There is no possibility of reversing the tide unless and until the faith of the New Testament is recaptured and the viewpoints of Christ and the apostles brought back to a place where they are foundational to evangelism. Without that, evangelism is superfluous and emptied of meaning.

The Work of Evangelism

Despite the current attacks on evangelism, there are multitudes of churches, individuals, and parachurch organizations who are doing the work of evangelism. Of church evangelism more will be said later. The media are saturating America by evangelistic outreach. On television we need only mention programs like those of Billy Graham, the 700 Club, PTL Club, Jerry Falwell, Rex Humbard, Oral Roberts, Robert Schuller, and others. FM radio stations owned by evangelicals flood the airwaves in every part of the United States. Shortwave radio broadcasts now blanket the earth with the gospel message.

Among the parachurch organizations are Campus Crusade for Christ, the InterVarsity Christian Fellowship, Child Evangelism, Young Life, Jews for Jesus, the American Tract Society, and a host of other organizations. The majority of these efforts are praiseworthy, and no one should render adverse judgment against the entire effort because of those whose activities do not live up to the ideal. The freedom of the airwaves can be abused. Zeal without knowledge and programs of low quality bring rightful criticism of the efforts of some whose sincerity cannot be questioned. Moreover, it cannot be denied that the freedom of speech in the area of religious programming has attracted some who are in it for the money, and who use their activities to fatten their own pocketbooks. Some broadcasters never render a report of their finances to the public. This has given rise to criticism and has even led to the creation of a policing organization which uses a sort of "Good Housekeeping" label to identify the legitimate agencies.

Some evangelistic efforts fail to emphasize the costly aspect of the Christian faith. Easy believism, cheap grace, and a soft-pedaling of Christian ethics can be detected. Sin is not looked upon as something abominable, so that among those who call themselves evangelicals conformity to the world, a growing divorce rate, bad business practices, and the absence of thinking Christianity can be seen. Pride in statistics marked by a rehearsal of the numbers of people converted, the high priority given to success measured in material terms, and a noticeable lack of toughheaded preaching centered on the scandal of the cross come across too readily.

Well-meaning people produce shoddy material, low grade radio broadcasts and telecasts, while others produce programs geared to the country-club mentality that bears the trademarks of secularity. Undue emphasis on divine healing (writing for handkerchiefs with the imprint of the healer's hand, which are supposed to carry healing power, and large-scale healing meetings in which close to one hundred percent of those who come to find relief from their afflictions go home disappointed) is rather commonplace. One glance at the Saturday religion section of the *Los Angeles Times* would convince anyone that all is not well in Zion.

In America one can detect a steady drift away from the Biblical view of redemption toward a pseudo-Freudian psychological approach to mental healing. Guilt is frequently looked upon as neurotic rather than real and is treated on the psychiatric sofa rather than the mourner's bench of the churches. The cymbals clang forth a message of positive thinking divorced from the tragic note of a Calvary on which a divine-human being was despised and rejected of men, His visage marred, His brow scored with the marks of the thorns, and His hands ripped by the nails that fastened His aching body to a crossbar. "I'm O.K., you're O.K." is a message that hides the awfulness of the Master's pronouncement, "In the world ye shall have tribulation." And this is a promise, not simply an aberrant possibility.

In spite of these criticisms we all do well to remember that numbers of God's people live a simple lifestyle, and with personal sacrifice adorn the gospel of Jesus Christ and are faithful even unto death. Men like Alexander Solzhenitsyn and Georgi Vins of the Soviet Union tell us something of the greatness of those whose spirit will not be quenched and whose fidelity continues despite persecution, imprisonment, and, as in the case of Solzhenitsyn, expatriation from the land he loves.

The Local Church, the Evangelistic Base

The simplest reading of the New Testament reveals that the evangelistic mandate was given to the church as a body of believers living in the world. We are not speaking here of the invisible church that constitutes all believers, living, dead, and those who will be part of that church in the future. We are speaking of an empirical entity with its bishops (elders) and deacons, its ordinances or sacraments, its worship and its fellowship. This is the church in the world with all of its weaknesses and strengths, its accomplishments and its follies, its hopes and its aspirations. It is the body to which believers should be attached and through which they are to work both within its confines and outside of them. For centuries the church has existed as a body broken up into segments we call the churches or denominations. Some who look upon division as an evil call for the visible, structural, organic union of the churches.

In America the movement to unite has included many of the major denominations under the badge of COCU. Very recently a plan of union has been devised which the churches involved in the effort will act upon in the months ahead. But any scheme for union may be nothing more than the bringing together of groups which no longer display any real evangelistic passion and which have been losing members in large numbers. In the past decade, depending on the reporting and the slightly varying years used, the decline in membership has been significant.

In a six-year period the United Methodist Church lost a million members. In ten years the United Presbyterian Church lost seven hundred thousand members. In seven years the Christian Church (Disciples of Christ) lost 563,000 members. In eight years the Protestant Episcopal Church lost 522,000 members. In seven years the United Church of Christ lost 211,000 members. Over a fifteen-year period the number of missionaries supported by the United Methodist Church shrank by two thirds, as did the task force of the United Presbyterian Church.

Some years ago the DOM (the missionary arm) of the National Council of Churches reported 12,500 missionaries supported by member denominations and several missionary agencies associated with the DOM whose denominations are not members of the NCC. Recently the DOM of the NCC reported that its missionary task overseas numbered approximately 5,000 people coming from churches with a membership of some thirty-eight million people. The Interdenominational Faith Mission Association and the Evangelical Foreign Missions Association report that their associated agencies support some thirteen thousand active missionaries representing a constituency which might number twelve to fifteen million people. These latter agencies are thoroughly orthodox in their theological beliefs and markedly evangelistic.

There is nothing in the current picture to warrant the claim that the major denominations in the National Council of Churches will become aggressively evangelistic in the days ahead. This does not mean there are not small groups in these denominations who are evangelistic. It is always possible that the Festival on Evangelism, which convenes in Kansas City in 1981, may spark a new interest in, and concern for, evangelism. Many of the larger denominations have expressed a desire to have a part in this festival, which has its rootage in the Lausanne Congress on World Evangelization, which convened in 1974. But unless this happens, the large denominations, excepting the Southern Baptist Convention and Lutheran Church-Missouri Synod, which stand outside the National Council of Churches, are not likely to become intensely interested in evangelism via the local congregations. In all probability the large denominations have in them many people who themselves are in need of evangelization. They will not get interested in evangelizing others until they have had an experience of conversion to Jesus Christ themselves.

The churches which are interested in evangelism are doing something about it. For example, the Coral Ridge Presbyterian Church of Fort Lauderdale, Florida has geared up its large congregation to engage in personal evangelism. Hundreds of people have been converted and have come into the fellowship of that church. Other churches around the nation have profited from this example and the ministry of its pastor in evangelism conferences. This church has stressed the role of the laity. Robert Schuller in Garden Grove, California, has done the same. The Peninsula Bible Church in Northern California has had a successful outreach. The Grace Chapel in Lexington, Massachusetts is growing rapidly through its evangelism outreach. Numbers of other local congregations around the country are vital and effective examples of this same kind of evangelistic outreach.

Members of many evangelical churches are engaged in what might be called Bible study class evangelism. Homes are opened to week night Bible classes, and unchurched neighbors are invited. These contacts lead to evangelistic outreach and invitations to become Christians through faith in Christ. These efforts have been quite productive. Moreover, personal evangelism among friends, in business, and by contacts with people in all of the avenues of life have been a useful means for reaching people with the gospel.

Curiously, local congregational evangelistic meetings seem to be a thing of the past for many churches. There was a time when more than twelve thousand evangelists held meetings in churches all around America. It was estimated then that more than a million people a day came under the hearing of the Word of God. Today the number of evangelists and local church revivals has been sharply reduced. Many churches do not have a church-centered evangelistic campaign at any time. The media of radio and television, and the rush of modern life, may account for this change. Local churches might be surprised by what they could do if they went back to congregation-centered evangelistic meetings on the church premises with the laity bringing in the unsaved to hear the gospel.

Mass evangelism is still an important method of evangelism. Bringing large numbers of people together has a unifying effect, opens the doors for those who would never attend a church, makes evangelism an event worthy of news coverage, and gives public witness to the power of the gospel. Billy Graham has been the key figure in mass evangelism for more than a quarter of a century. But this form of evangelism requires the services of men who are specially gifted and hard to find. Before Billy Graham's day, God used Charles E. Fuller in a great way. When Mr. Graham's work has ended, God may well raise up someone else who is not known to us now, but who is being readied by the Holy Spirit for that moment.

The greatest thing that could happen to the churches today would be for them to get back on the evangelistic track. They would replace the members they had lost, increase the numbers of their churches, expand their financial base, and open doors for renewed outreach beyond the confines of the American continent. God speed the day when this will happen!

Conclusion

We know from the history of spiritual awakenings around the

world that the Holy Spirit works sovereignly from time to time to bring refreshing newness to the people of God and to expand the number of members of the body of Christ. The great awakening in America in the eighteenth century profoundly affected the colonies and later the republic. Another such awakening is not an impossibility. It can take place. The history of the church has been marked by ups and downs, just as there were ups and downs in the history of Israel. In some parts of the world, such as Africa, it is claimed that if the present rate of increase in the church members continues that continent will be predominantly Christian by the end of this century. But this must be seen against the larger picture that countries in Europe which once were thoroughly Christian have now become mission fields. Scandinavia, Germany, France, England, Italy, and the low countries are vast mission fields today. These nations need to be reached and only evangelism will do the job.

It is also important to remind ourselves that the Holy Spirit is the person responsible for converting the unsaved. Our responsibility is to be good stewards by doing what God commands us through Scripture. Faithfulness, not results, is what counts. The harvest is always preceded by plowing, planting, and fertilizing. But it is the Holy Spirit who sends the latter rain and brings forth an abundant harvest.

The signs of the times suggest the soon coming of Christ. The period before that advent will be marked by apostasy, coldness of heart, and grave troubles. But it will also be marked by a gracious ingathering of souls into God's kingdom. And this always comes about when the people of God do what they have been called to do—evangelize. The threefold price of evangelism is: (1) commitment by the people of God to the Lordship of Christ; (2) doing what Scripture requires to be filled with the Holy Spirit of God; and (3) surrendering anything that would keep them from fulfilling the will of God for the church, which is to preach the gospel of Jesus Christ to all the world.

The Electric Church

by Ben Armstrong

Twisting the dial of a borrowed television set, a desperate young man was looking for a program that would distract him from his agony.

"I had already decided to end my life by driving my motorcycle into a wall. I had lost everything—my job, my wife, my kid—because of drinking and drugs," Brad Raymond recalls. "That day I had taken more drugs than ever. I wanted to get myself stoned so high that I wouldn't know what I was doing. Just to fill in time until the high started, I was turning the TV dial, hoping to find some rock music. Accidentally, I stumbled across a Chicago station that I had never come across before. What stopped me was a guy with a guitar singing a quiet song. He was Barry McGuire. His record 'The Eve of Destruction' had been the theme song of the sixties. I could relate to him. Now he was singing about Jesus, saying that Jesus was waiting for me. For me? I had spent twenty-four years rebelling against my family, running away, dealing in drugs. It made me wonder. Could I have the hope he was singing about? I'd tried drugs, alcohol, women, money. But I'd never given Jesus a chance. Maybe He was the answer. I prayed, *Lord, if you can, change my life.* Right away there was a deep sense of peace. Instead of ending my life, that night was the start of a new life. The next morning I wanted to get out of the rooming house and away from the drug scene. I found myself drawn to a building with a big cross. It turned out to be Pacific Garden Mission, and one of their counselors helped me to understand what had happened the night before. As the counselor talked to me, I remembered that my dad had listened to the Pacific Garden Mission radio program *Unshackled*. In fact, he became a Christian through that program. And here, ten years later, I had just met Jesus Christ myself through a TV program on a Christian station!"

Brad Raymond, who now is a member of my staff at National Religious Broadcasters and has four years experience as a volunteer prison chaplain, is one of thousands who owe their lives to religious broadcasts. One ministry alone, the nationwide *700 Club*, receives approximately 4,000 telephone calls a year from people who are on the verge of suicide. In 1979 the *700 Club* received 1.4 million telephone calls from people seeking all types of spiritual counsel. Almost 100,000 of these called to report that the program had led them to give their lives to Christ.[1]

These people are part of an exciting new fellowship, which started at an evening vesper service January 2, 1921. That service, in a prestigious church in Pittsburgh, Pennsylvania, sowed the seeds for a tremendous transformation of American church life. Today, six decades after the historic evening when Calvary Episcopal Church made the first religious broadcast over pioneer radio station KDKA, virtually every church in the nation feels the effects of religious broadcasting.

Paralleling the pervasive influence of the broadcast media upon American life in general, religious radio and television are now part of the American scene. In an average week the number of people who hear a religious message by radio or television is far greater than the total attendance at all of the nation's churches. Church attendance averages 41 percent, while more than 47 percent of all adults hear or see at least one religious broadcast per week.[2]

With more than 8,000 radio stations in the United States, about 1,000 stations—or one out of eight—offer at least 14 hours a week of religious material. Approximately 600 stations offer religious programs and music virtually full time. Religious television stations are operating in most major markets, and hundreds of secular television stations across the country are presenting a wide variety of religious programs. According to *Time* magazine, TV industry executives say "there is no apparent saturation point in sight."[3] In addition to TV programs "popping up at an incredible rate" on secular stations, the religious media are multiplying with one new religious radio station going on the air every week and one new TV station every month.

Thanks to radio and television, almost 130 million Americans a week hear the gospel message. Special programs, such as a Billy Graham Crusade telecast, frequently gather audiences of more than 50 million people. In addition, millions throughout the world hear the gospel from superpower international radio stations operated by American believers. Never before in the history of the world has it been possible to take the message of Jesus Christ to so many people. Radio has the capacity to cut across man-made barriers of all kinds—including geographical boundaries, language differences, iron curtains, and double-bolted apartment doors. Even people who live beyond the reach of electricity and other technological amenities have a link to the world through low-cost transistor radios. Today millions who cannot read can hear the gospel in their own language via transistor radio. Communications satellites open the intriguing possibility that in the near future it will be possible for everyone on earth to both hear and see an event instantaneously.

Could this be a fulfillment of Revelation 1:7, when the Lord Jesus will return "and every eye shall see him"? In a conversation with Karl Barth, the famous theologian, David De Plessis identified the broadcast media with the angel of Revelation 14:6, 7 flying "in the midst of heaven, having the everlasting gospel to preach unto them that dwell on the earth, and to every nation, and kindred, and tongue, and people." Are the broadcast media the works of men, or are they modern miracles, given to us in the twentieth century as part of the unfolding of God's plan for eternity?

A New Concept of the Church

The unprecedented linking of twentieth-century technology with Christ's commandment to "Go ye into all the world, and preach the gospel to every creature" (Mark 16:15) has created a dynamic new phenomenon that I call "the electric church."

The concept of the electric church came to me in the winter of 1973, on an airplane trip to Chicago. Attempting to land under very poor weather conditions, the airplane circled above Chicago in total blackness. When the plane finally broke through the dense cloud cover, the lights of the city suddenly appeared below.

Those thousands of sparkling pinpoints piercing the expanse of blackness presented a beautiful sight. The contrast between the intensely shining points of light and the surrounding blackness formed a modern illustration of John 1:5, "The light shines in the darkness, and the darkness has not overcome it" *(Revised Standard Version)*.

Even in today's spiritual darkness, I thought, religious broadcasting is beaming the light of the gospel. Each of the lights below seemed to represent a radio or television station tower raised up by God. He promises in John 12:32 that when Jesus is lifted up all mankind will be drawn to Him. These station towers are lifting up Jesus and drawing people from all walks of life to Him, the true Light, I thought. Then I realized that the radio and TV towers are merely structures used to transmit the gospel, the message that encourages each believer to become a beam of light in a dark world. The men, women, boys, and girls who live in God's light are the members of the true church. For the first time I saw the lights below as millions of religious broadcasting listeners and viewers and as the members of a great and new manifestation of the church created by God for this age—the electric church.

In this vision I understood that the religious broadcasting audience is indeed a revolutionary new form of the worshiping, witnessing church that existed twenty centuries ago. In New Testament times the members of the church gathered in homes, shared the Scriptures, prayed together, praised God for the gift of His Son Jesus Christ, and testified to His presence in their lives. They were on fire for the Lord, and their lives had been changed by Him. As a result they changed the world.

Radio and television have broken through the walls of tradition and have restored conditions remarkably similar to the early church. In the electric church, as in New Testament times, worship once again takes place in the home. The speaker is the guest, as was the apostle Paul who traveled to people's homes. As a guest the radio or television minister earns the right to be heard by the content of his message. Reversing the long-established roles between the person in the pulpit and the person in the pew, the leadership role in the electric church does not belong to the radio or television speaker—not even a Billy Graham or a Jerry Falwell. The real leader is the individual who has the power to turn the dial and thereby to wipe out the image or sound of the program in a second. Similarly, the first evangelists and teachers, and the people whom they visited, came together as equals. All were people who had personally found Christ. In New Testament times, visiting evangelists and teachers were expected to bring a message from the Scriptures, which listeners could then apply to the needs of their lives. The book of Acts tells us that Paul, Peter, Stephen, and others chosen by God spoke not in their own power but through the power of the Holy Spirit. That's what made their message dynamic, bringing as many as three thousand listeners into the community of Christ in a single day!

What is the essential ingredient, the power that links the messenger and the hearer? Isn't it the transforming power of the Holy Spirit transmitted through the spoken Word of God to the listener? That is the power that brings the electric church into being. The electric church is not a manifestation of modern technology but of the power of the Holy Spirit. Through the broadcast media the local assembly of believers is able to reach out, to transmit the good news to others. Far from supplanting the local church, the electric church enlarges, enhances, extends, and complements it. All believers who beam God's message over the broadcast media and all who hear that message are part of the electric church.

At the time of my discovery of the electric church concept, I had been in religious broadcasting for two decades. But until the revelation that came with the vision of the city lights against the darkness, I had not been fully aware of the presence and power of the electric church. Only then did I grasp the authentic meaning of what God is doing with the broadcast media.

A Revolution Catches Fire

The electric church has launched a revolution as dramatic as the revolution that began when Martin Luther nailed his ninety-five theses to the cathedral door at Wittenberg. Just as the Reformation brought sweeping changes in the way Christians understood their relationship to God and the way they expressed their devotion through worship, so has the electric church.

My new understanding of the electric church was a revelation that I wanted to bring to the attention of everyone who cares about communicating the gospel. The first public presentation was in 1976 at the annual convention of National Religious Broadcasters, held that year in conjunction with the National Association of Evangelicals. Addressing this Washington, D.C. convocation of religious broadcasters and church leaders who maintain the classical beliefs of Christianity, I introduced the concept of the electric church. Identifying it as a grass roots movement called into existence by God for the age in which we live, I shared my conviction that His purpose is to use the electric church to revitalize the older forms of the churches, empowering them to keep up with the challenges of a rapidly expanding population and a rapidly diminishing time span before the return of Jesus Christ.

The response to the speech seemed positive, but as time went on I became aware of some reluctance to accept this concept of a revolutionary dynamic new force at work in the world today. This kind of reaction to a new idea should not have been surprising. At an earlier NRB convention, Marhsall McLuhan, one of the world's best known commentators on communications theory, had told us that "if you didn't understand radio and television you couldn't understand the twentieth century."

Ever since January 2, 1921, when the senior pastor of Calvary Episcopal Church decided that radio was not worth his time and assigned his junior assistant to lead the evening vesper service which became history's first religious broadcast, there have been church leaders who were disinterested in the potential of broadcasting and church leaders who wanted to explore it. Disinterest later changed into strong negative feelings about the use of radio and television for the communication of the gospel. This negativism may stem largely from an emotional or psychological preference for the printed word versus the spoken or visual word of television, according to James A. Taylor, managing editor of *The Journal of the United Church of Canada*. In an article for *The Christian Century* (April 20, 1977), he draws a parallel between today's liberal churches and the church of Rome at the time of the Reformation. Pointing out that the entrenched theology of liberalism faces a technological revolution comparable to the "invention of printing, which put the Scriptures into the hands of the laity," he believes that just as "the Reformation was the child of printing," so today's born-again movement "is a child of television." Taylor concludes that the chasm between evangelicals and "the older liberal churches goes beyond differences" in theological interpretations of Scripture, sin, and salvation to "differences in perception rooted in their parent technologies."

Almost nobody is neutral about broadcasting, particularly television, and almost everybody has intense feelings about "the church." There are almost as many different definitions of the church as there are churchgoers. It's not surprising then that the phrase "the electric church" sent shock waves through the leadership ranks of American religious institutions.

Theologian Martin Marty of the University of Chicago welcomed the appearance of the phrase "the electric church" as a name for the "invisible religion" that he had long opposed. An articulate and prolific critic of religious radio and television, Dr. Marty paints a picture of "Mr. and Mrs. Invisible Religion" being entertained by "ruffle-shirted, pink-tuxedoed men" and "celebrity women who talk about themselves under the guise of born-again autobiographies." According to Dr. Marty, the glamour of religious telecasts sets up an unrealistic basis of comparison with the church "down the block" and its "off-key choirs, sweaty and homely people" and "ordinary pastors."[4]

In the same vein William F. Fore of the National Council of Churches (NCC) insists, "What worries me is whether this electronic church is in fact pulling people away from the local church, whether it is substituting an anonymous and therefore undemanding commitment for the kind of person-to-person involvement and group commitment that is the essence of the local church." The head of the NCC Communications Commission maintains that "it is relatively easy to raise funds through radio and TV, but it is almost impossible to channel that kind of support and interest back into a local church."[5]

Dr. Fore, as a spokesman for an important group of American churches, touches the points where some churches are hurting today. Membership trends during the past decade help to explain the current uneasiness over the electric church, according to sociologist Jeffrey K. Hadden. Noting that "mainline Protestant churches have experienced incipient decline while conservative churches have continued" to grow, he emphasizes the "phenomenal growth" of religious broadcasting and underscores the fact that Christian radio and television are "predominantly utilized and controlled by evangelicals."

Explaining the significance of these trends, the Baylor University sociologist cites the historical background:

For a long time, perhaps since the Scopes trial in 1925, the Eastern secular and liberal Protestant establishments treated evangelical religion as if it were an archaic religious form, peculiarly persistent in some regions of the country, but not a significant factor in American culture.

During the 1970's a whole series of developments drew attention to the importance of evangelicals in American culture. Perhaps none was more significant than candidate Jimmy Carter's openness about his religious faith. During that same year, George Gallup discovered that fifty million adults claimed they were "born-again" Christians.[6]

The news media immediately declared that 1977 was "the year of the evangelical." Dr. Hadden prefers to describe it as "the year in which non-evangelicals discovered the existence of a very large sector of American society, previously presumed to be an insignificant fringe."

Time and *Newsweek,* devoting cover stories to the born-again movement, reported that it stretched from the White House and university campuses to factories and farms.[7] To the secular media it was remarkable that spiritual concerns could matter to millions of men and women who came from the mainstream of American life. *Time* and *Newsweek* sought in their comprehensive articles for an explanation of how this could be happening in today's world. Their research pointed to religious radio and television as an active, forceful influence. Coming by an entirely different path, they too had discovered the electric church.

The New York Times in a 1978 feature article observed that "as the ranks of born-again evangelicals have swelled, their call to convert the world to Christ has translated itself into an ever larger and more complex pattern of religious broadcasts." The nation's most authoritative newspaper credited religious broadcasting with bringing born-again believers together on the common ground of shared faith. This "unifying process" had spurred the growth of the movement, according to religion editor Kenneth Briggs. The chief tool, he pointed out, was religious television, which "makes it possible to galvanize this diverse sweep of Christians into a much more uniform, homogeneous constituency in which such matters as denominational identity mean far less than they ever did in the past." What did matter to born-again Christians, the *Times* editor remarked, was "to save souls from perdition." Accordingly, religious broadcasts gave first priority to pleading with the listener for a "change of heart."[8]

Lacking the background of *The New York Times* editor, many secular journalists found both the content and the purpose of religious programs bewildering. Particularly baffling was the appeal for funds and the emphasis on "winning people to Christ."

Coming from a different perspective, the video journalists on *Sixty Minutes* and *20/20* had problems concerning the genuineness of the people on the religious programs and the possible benefits to the people in the audience. Many members of the mass media posed a barrage of questions about money and motives. The fascination of the secular news media with religious broadcasting coincided with another vogue of the late 70's, when investigative reporting was the dominant style of the "post-Watergate era." Even the Billy Graham Association, one of the most respected and best managed ministries in Christian broadcasting, became a target for unfounded charges of financial manipulation. Organizations such as the *PTL Club*, suffering from various management problems that were the inevitable byproducts of rapid growth, underwent massive assaults from the news media. While some secular journalists seemed to use these stories as opportunities to express their own distaste for Biblical religion, their reports did serve to awaken legitimate concerns among sincere Christians.

Dissension in the Ranks

The Southern California Council of Churches and the UCLA Department of Religion sponsored a symposium in December 1978 to consider "the effects of the electric church on the citizens of California." By the time of the meeting, the atmosphere was heavy from the shocking events that had happened only two weeks before in Jonestown, Guyana, where the leader of a religious cult from California had assassinated a California Congressman and a news reporter, and then had persuaded or coerced more than 900 men, women, and children to join him in a grisly mass suicide. One of the psychiatrists at the UCLA symposium declared that if Jim Jones had used radio and television there would have been "millions of deaths." As a participant in the symposium, I felt that my contribution was to take its focus away from the area of speculation and to focus instead on the real role that religious broadcasting has played in strengthening America's churches. Most impressive to the Los Angeles Times was my concept of the electric church as a grass-roots movement, maintained by the people in the pews rather than imposed by a self-anointed leader like Jim Jones or by some ecclesiastical authority. Southern California abounds with radio and television programs produced by local churches, Christian radio and TV stations (including Trinity Television Network, which beams religious programs by satellite), and scores of nationally distributed programs. In radio alone, several programs have ministered to audiences in the United States and overseas for more than four decades. A partial list includes such favorites as *Haven of Rest, Thru the Bible* with J. Vernon McGee, *Morning Sunshine* with Ralph Neighbour, and *Lutheran Gospel Hour* with Pastor J. Norheim. The area's largest churches—Hollywood First Presbyterian, Calvary Chapel of Costa Mesa, Melodyland, and Garden Grove Community Church—all have broadcast ministries. Garden Grove's *Hour of Power* with Robert Schuller reaches four million viewers across the nation every week, making an impressive outreach for a local congregation of 8,000 members.[9]

The outstanding success of *Hour of Power* has brought Dr. Schuller a steady stream of criticism, not only from secular journalists but increasingly from other ministries. Critics from both the liberal and the conservative ranks have raised questions about his theology, his style, and the spread of his ministry. When Dr. Schuller spoke at the 1979 convention of National Religious Broadcasters, reiterating his evangelical beliefs and sharing his experience as a communicator of the gospel, some broadcasters hailed it as a high point of the convention and others deplored it as a concession to worldly success. At the same convention, Commissioner James H. Quello of the Federal Communications Commission expressed his personal gratitude to religious broadcasters for carrying the gospel into the homes of America. The Commissioner revealed that his own son had returned to the Lord as a result of watching *Hour of Power*.

What happens to born-again viewers like the Commissioner's son? Do they continue, as some churchmen charge, to "worship by tube" with "the living-room sofa supplanting the pew and gifts mailed to televangelists ... taking the place of Sunday offerings"?[10] Or do they follow the pattern of first century believers who were on fire to tell others about the Lord Jesus Christ? Why is there such a gap between the numbers of people attending church services and the numbers tuning in to religious broadcasts? The difference is too wide to include only those people prevented from attending church by illness or advanced age. Are some people missing the total message from the gospel broadcasters?

Billy Graham ends almost every crusade telecast by urging viewers, "Go to church this Sunday." Many prominent radio speakers, such as Theodore Epp, J. Vernon McGee, and John

D. Jess devote a portion of their daily broadcasts to underscoring the importance of joining a local church and participating in its life. Robert Schuller claims that his favorite letters come from people who say that they are no longer able to watch his program because they now attend worship services at a church near home. Every reputable electric church practitioner agrees that his work is not over until the listener or viewer becomes part of a local church. Reaching the unchurched is an urgent priority for every organization holding membership in National Religious Broadcasters. Some nationally syndicated programs reach out to the unchurched through personal follow-up by local churches of various denominations. The idea of local follow-ups originated with denominational broadcasts. At the community level Christian radio stations guide callers to neighborhood churches where they will find a warm welcome and an opportunity to grow spiritually. The Moody stations in the Moody Radio Network and Family Radio Network are outstanding in this effort.

Most of the vast religious radio-TV audience seems to be heeding the broadcaster's advice. Church attendance in the United States is considerably higher than in Great Britain and Western Europe. Significantly these countries have relatively little gospel programming on their state-operated radio and television systems. Few of their programs are either evangelical or evangelistic, although there are encouraging signs of change. The correlation between Christian broadcasting and church attendance is obvious. During the past fifty years religious life in Great Britain and Europe has declined precipitously. By comparison religion in America has remained remarkably stable during this past half century of economic depression, war, and social upheaval.

Religious radio and television programming is the unique distinction which makes American Christianity different from its overseas counterparts.

Many of today's evangelical leaders grew up listening to the powerful messages of Walter Maier on *The Lutheran Hour*, Charles Fuller on *Old Fashioned Revival Hour*, Donald Grey Barnhouse, and Paul Rader. Two examples of leaders who can testify to the impact of radio messages on their lives are D. James Kennedy of Coral Ridge Presbyterian Church (Fort Lauderdale, Florida) and Jerry Falwell of Thomas Road Baptist Church (Lynchburg, Virginia). Both now use the broadcast media to carry the gospel message beyond the confines of their church buildings.

Obviously the churches that have a stake in broadcasting, either through direct sponsorship of programs or through follow-up activities, have reaped the greatest and most direct benefits from evangelical radio and television. Naturally, people who have been moved by gospel broadcasts seem to have joined evangelical churches, where the sermons, Bible teaching, and basic theological approach are similar to what they've heard on the air. The growth of evangelical churches in recent years is one of the most significant developments in the nation's religious life. Concurrently, membership in mainline churches whose leadership espouses liberal theology has declined steadily.

For clergymen facing empty pews, shrinking membership rolls, and dwindling budgets, the rising popularity of evangelical radio and television suggests that religious broadcasting is the enemy. Bolstering that point of view is a steady barrage from executives in major denominations, particularly from executives who are experts in communications. In the past decade they have competed with other denominational departments to capture a small portion of the reduced funds now coming to national headquarters. At the same time they have lost their hold on the nation's airwaves, obtaining less airtime for liberal presentations even as evangelical time zoomed.

The situation "has every hallmark of an intensifying war of survival among battling Christian groups" with "not even a remote basis for reconciliation" in sight, according to psychologist Robert M. Liebert, who traces the origins of the war to the long-standing rift between the liberal and evangelical churches.[11]

Almost since the advent of radio, liberal and evangelical churchmen have taken different approaches to religious broadcasting. These differences eventually led to the formation of National Religious Broadcasters in 1944. Free and complete access to the broadcast media, in both sustaining time and purchased time, is one of the basic tenets of NRB. Until 1979 the liberal leaders of the National Council of Churches adhered to a stern stance against the purchase of time for religious programs.[12]

Looking at the Facts

Gospel broadcasts can give the undecided person spiritual support and psychological reinforcement. The experience of many evangelical denominations offers clear evidence that religious radio and television acts as a recruiting agency for the local church. Additionally, Christian broadcasts help to strengthen the faith of the 130 million listeners and viewers of the electric church, thereby strengthening the local churches in which they participate. Some theorists criticize religious broadcasters, oddly enough, for beaming more programs to the person who is active in the church rather than the one who is still outside the church. According to *Time* magazine, one executive of a major denomination "complained that broadcast preachers were infecting his parishes with fundamentalism."[13] Acknowledging that some mainline denominations equate fundamentalism with the electric church and its "simple faith, believing, contributing $25 a month to save souls," psychologist Robert Liebert observes that "the general public has never equated Christianity with social activism in the way presumed by liberal theologians." The charge that religious radio and television fail to preach "the whole gospel" is echoed by some arch-conservative critics in the evangelical camp.

Nevertheless, the critics grudgingly admit that people participate in the electric church because religious radio and television programs are fulfilling their deepest needs. Edwin Diamond of MIT, who dislikes and distrusts Christian television, acknowledges that spiritual hunger "as well as materialistic and entertainment cravings" makes many religious TV viewers feel that going "to church on Sunday morning and to prayer meeting on Wednesday night ... isn't enough." Reporting that these churchgoers "want the Christian message in between times as well," he adds that "they feel the need for God's television as surely as they need food or sleep."[14]

The craving for spiritual food prompts the typical religious radio listener to leave the radio dial permanently tuned to a religious station. In survey after survey, the favorite weekday offerings on religious stations are Bible-teaching programs on the order of *Back to the Bible* with Theodore Epp, *Chapel of the Air* with John D. Jess and David Mains, *Radio Bible Class* with Richard De Haan, and *Encounter* with Stephen Olford. Millions enroll in the Bible study correspondence courses that supplement the broadcasts of these teachers and other radio-TV speakers. Responding to this need for a deeper understanding of the Word of God, the Sunday School Board of the Southern Baptist Convention has developed a multimedia effort that utilizes broadcasts, print, and local church involvement. The television component, *At Home With the Bible*, proves that it is possible to present serious, challenging material on the home screen. Approximately 100,000 people a year write in for the intensive study course offered on the program. More and more teaching programs will appear on religious television in the years ahead, experts predict, with the growth of Christian TV stations fostering the development of a wide range of programs for specific audiences, as in Christian radio.

Is this emphasis on the broadcast media diverting dollars away from the local church and its work? The statistics indicate that in the audiences of the major religious broadcasters, somewhere between five and ten percent of the viewers and listeners send in some financial support during the course of a year. The average gift ranges from $5 to $10. For every $1 gift to a broadcast organization, the average donor gives $4 to the local church, according to a national study conducted by an independent research firm. Of the donors questioned in the study, 20 percent say they are more active in church affairs as a result of listening to religious programs, ten percent say they are less active, and the majority indicate no change.

Critics and Advocates

Research data from any source does not quell criticism from those whose ministries are affected adversely by the rising trend of evangelical strength. This was apparent at a consultation on the "electronic church" sponsored by the communications commission of the National Council of Churches, the communications department of the United States Catholic Conference and New York University. Colin Williams, former dean of Yale Divinity School, chose to ignore the statistics presented by Pat Robertson, president of the Christian Broadcasting Network and host of *The 700 Club*, which helps bring 75,000 new members a year into various local churches across the country. Dr. Williams dismissed the presentation for its "simplistic" theology, which he compared to the "weak theology" of a Billy Graham Crusade. Similarly, responding to my talk on federal regulation of radio and television, Father Donald Mathews of Fordham University said that "protecting religion on the air" was a minor concern to him and his ecumenical associates in the Telecommunications Consumer Coalition.

According to the office of news and information of the National Council of Churches, the "electronic church" consultation in February 1980 showed that "problems with television" were basically "a rehash of the age-old conflict between liberal Christian theology" and conservative evangelicals. Theologian Richard McBrien of Boston College detected a new variation. He saw the two contemporary opponents as Bible-believing or "neo-fundamentalist Protestants and neo-fundamentalist Catholics" versus liberal or "mainline Protestant and mainline Catholics." The NCC summary stated that "the medium of television—so well suited to and used by conservative evangelists—has suddenly tipped the scales."[15]

The New York Times went further, declaring that "the electronic church is turning more people on." *The Times* reported that the electronic church consultation marked a shift in the attitudes of "the traditional churches," which "once looked paternally and perhaps contemptuously" at evangelical broadcasts.[16] Religion editor Kenneth Briggs described religious broadcasting as "a $1 billion yearly business" and National Religious Broadcasters as "an umbrella organization for television and radio evangelical groups," which has grown from 104 members fifteen years ago to 900 today. Examining data from the Gallup study on the unchurched, Mr. Briggs observed, "Someone is providing doctrine to this expanding proportion of the population." His feature article quoted positive statements about religious broadcasting from sociologist Jeffrey K. Hadden of Baylor University, who indicated "the electronic church may be more successful in attracting those who have drifted away from church participation rather than new converts." The article concluded that evangelical broadcasters have utilized technology to grasp a "crucial" opportunity to communicate the gospel, fully aware that the opportunity is limited because radio-TV programs do not "fulfill all the functions of a local church." Television speaker Robert Schuller, who is an authority on church growth, told the consultation that broadcast ministries were "no substitute for the genuine community and care provided by vital local churches."

The liberal churchmen attending the consultation apparently failed to hear its basic message. According to theologian Richard McBrien, "It is self evident that the churches should be using the electronic media to communicate the gospel."[17] Psychologist Robert M. Liebert urged the liberal churches to "get their act together," by making "more and better use of TV themselves" and buying airtime. He concluded:

If the Mainline churches do in fact have spiritual significance for their people then this fact can be advertised, dramatized, and revitalized through the same media that have served The Electronic Denominations so well. . . . If there is a Christian way of life missed by The Electronic Denominations, and if this way of life is the way to salvation and peace, then it is certainly time to find better ways of spreading the word.

The general secretary of United Methodist Communications, Curtis A. Chambers, agrees that "responsible religious groups indeed must use the electronic media" to express "religious convictions and ethical commitments." In order to be "faithful to the mandate of the gospel," Dr. Chambers advocates more church support for the electronic media. He points out, "The United Methodist Church, because of its presence in neighborhoods all across the country, is in a unique place to wed the tremendous power of radio and television with the caring, ministering, warm-hearted community of faith which ideally is the essence of every local church."[18]

The Enemy Strikes

The overwhelming evidence is that churches of all types appreciate the freedom we have in the United States to broadcast Christian programs. In 1974, when religious broadcasting faced a serious threat, churches across the country swung into action, setting off an avalanche of mail to the Federal Communications Commission.

The threat originated with two radio station owners, Jeremy Lansman and Lorenzo Milam. They had tried unsuccessfully to obtain a station license in Spokane, Washington, losing out to the radio network operated by Moody Bible Institute of Chicago. Lansman and Milam filed a petition with the FCC, seeking to stop the licensing of religious stations in the educational FM band. The petition vehemently attacked the programming of WMBI, the Moody Radio station in Chicago. Citizen reaction against this petition was immediate, emphatic, and unprecedented. Letters poured into the FCC, overturning all previous records. Some journalists now claim that the tons of mail resulted from a peculiar form of mass hysteria. That's hardly true. What prompted the letters in the first place was a natural reaction of outrage brought on by the attack and by the sacrilegious tone of the Lansman-Milam petition.

Adding fuel to the fire, Lorenzo Milam later filed another document pertaining to RM-2493 giving his view of the broadcasts on WMBI. In one passage he charged:

> For 24 hours they begged, pleaded, demanded, asked, requested, intoned, suggested, whispered that I should come to Christ. For 24 hours, without surcease (except for some tawdry UPI newsflashes and stories), without pause, without interruption, without any hesitation they told me of the happiness of Christ's world, the delights of the Bible, the pleasure of being a Christian, in love with a Christian god, the joy of being washed in the Blood of the Lamb. For 24 hours they chatted pleasantly about Him, about what He would mean to me, gave me friendly advice about The Lord's Way (which they saw, which they could give to me, if I wanted it); they told me of Hope for my Soul if I would get right with God and abandon my naughty ways. Intermixed with the voices were the songs. Dear God, the songs! I was washed in verses, rhythms, voices, dances, foot tappings that told me more about God, and Christ, and The Cross, and His Sacrifices for Us, and Me.
>
> For 24 hours I was jingled and jangled in the voices—not unlike Dean Martin or Judy Collins or Perry Como or Doris Day or Brazil 66—nonstop singing, Fox Trot, Mambo, E-Z Listenin' 2/4 time melodies of His love, His Word, His Flesh, His Sacrifice, His Need for Me, My Need for Him, Everyone's Need for Salvation.
>
> I thought I should weep with the sheer tedium of it. It was a warm, tiny, cloying, nonstop peek into a very limited, narrow, miniscule vision of Man and his Godhead. It was a single, telescopic vision of religion: one based entirely on Back-to-the-Bible Christian Fundamental Religion; ignoring by definition 98 percent of the world's religious thinking.
>
> What we were getting from WMBI was nothing more or less than a single long diatribe for the Moody World View—a fulltime, ongoing, nonstop, endless, open-ended 24 hours, seven day a week, 52 week year, year after year commercial for the Moody Bible Institute, their pinhole view of humanity, and their dank view of the Divine.[19]

It's no wonder that NRB saw this attack as antireligious and that Christians across the country began expressing their opinions to the FCC. Mail opposing the Lansman-Milam petition amounted to seven hundred thousand pieces by August 1975, when the commission ruled in favor of FM educational religious stations. Letters continued to pour in even after the favorable ruling. The NRB, religious radio stations, and the secular press launched an intensive effort to tell the public that religious broadcasting was no longer threatened by petition RM 2493. Eventually the volume of letters against the Lansman-Milam petition dwindled to seven thousand a day. By the end of 1979 more than ten million pieces of mail had come to the FCC about the petition.

While the continuing stream of mail after the decision, from well-intentioned but uninformed citizens, has become a nuisance to the FCC staff and a potential embarrassment to religious broadcasters, it has positive aspects. First, it is a dramatic indication of how intensely Americans cherish our national heritage of religious freedom. Second, it is a dramatic indication of the people's high regard for religious broadcasting. The reason for this strong emotional attachment seems to be expressed best in a statement from a media executive who described a local station as "part of people's daily religious life." Her fond description, which happened to have been inspired by WMBI, applies as warmly and appropriately to hundreds of religious stations across the country that faithfully present the timeless truths of the Bible. How could anyone, cynic or believer, doubt the reality or validity of the electric church in today's world?

[1]"CBN Counseling Centers Receive Record 1.4 Million Telephone Calls," News release from CBN (Virginia Beach, Virginia), December 21, 1979.

[2]Ben Armstrong, *The Electric Church* (Nashville, Tennessee: Thomas Nelson, Inc., 1979), p. 7.

[3]"Stars of the Cathode Church," *Time* (February 4, 1980), p. 64.

[4]Martin Marty, quoted by William F. Fore in a speech, "Is Anybody Listening and Why?" given before Broadcasters Council, Seventh-Day Adventist Church, Oxnard, California, August 21, 1978.

[5]Fore, *op. cit.*

[6]Jeffrey K. Hadden, "Some Sociological Reflections on the Electronic Church," speech at Electronic Church Consultation, New York University, February 6-7, 1980.

[7]"Back to That Oldtime Religion," *Time* (December 26, 1977), pp. 52-58; and "Born Again!" Newsweek (October 25, 1976), pp. 68-78.

[8]Kenneth A. Briggs, "Religious Broadcasting: The Fourth Network," New York Times, January 29, 1978, p. 18E.

[9]Armstrong, *op. cit.*, pp. 111-115.

[10]"Stars of the Cathode Church, *Time* (February 4, 1980), p. 64.

[11]Robert M. Liebert, "The Electronic Church: A Psychological Perspective," speech at Electronic Church Consultation, February 6-7, 1980.

[12]"NCC OKs Paid Time," *Religious Broadcasting.*

[14]*Time, loc. cit.*

[14]Edwin Diamond, "God's Television," *American Film* (March, 1980), p. 30.

[15]National Council of Churches news release, "Mainline Churches Debate Response to Electronic Church" (February 11, 1980).

[16]Kenneth A. Briggs, "The Electronic Church Is Turning More People On," *New York Times,* February 10, 1980.

[17]Richard P. O'Brien, "The Electronic Church: A Catholic Theologian's Perspective," speech at Electronic Church Consultation, February 6-7, 1980.

[18]Curtis A. Chambers, letter to Editor, the *Dayton Daily News,* January 27, 1979; and an unpublished letter to the Editor of *Arkansas Methodist.*

[19]The document was filed with the FCC, June 2, 1975, in response to opposition to RM-2493.

Christian Celebrities: Media Hype in the Church

by John MacArthur and Gary Inrig

Whatever happened to true spirituality? Why is it that in the Christian church today it has become so popular to exalt all the wrong people for all the wrong reasons? Why is it that we are exposed, through books, programs, and public meetings, to a parade of personalities and celebrities whose stories are held before us as models to be imitated or experiences to be sought?

In the Christian media we hear far more about new converts who are famous stars, singers, athletes, and politicians than we ever do about mature Christians living holy lives or about godly individuals who are faithfully, and often sacrificially, preaching the Word of God. These new Christians, whom the Bible calls "spiritual babies," are promoted and publicized until Christians all over the country are eager to make available to them every possible pulpit and platform. Over and over they tell their stories or perform their acts but, inevitably, such occasions are characterized by a pervasive superficiality. It is hardly their fault. After all, how could they be expected to speak with wisdom and maturity when they have been believers for only a short time, and when all they are expected to know is the account of their own conversion? Too often such believers are not encouraged to move on in Christian growth and to share the results of a maturing walk with the Lord Jesus. One pro football player recounts how, for eight years, he repeated the same story over and over, because he needed nothing more. And in retelling the same story, there is a great temptation to enhance the story. Sins become more lurid and conversions more dramatic. The result is an exciting but shallow performance, but we could hardly expect a solid grasp of Biblical truth or a true discernment in spiritual matters from mere babies. But why has the evangelical church allowed itself to be caught up in this Hollywood syndrome of the glamorous and the spectacular? Granted, not all Christian celebrities are spiritually immature and many are completely sincere. We can thank God for what He is doing in such people's lives, but this hardly removes the need for a careful examination of practices which are seriously detrimental, not only to the celebrity Christian himself, but even more so to the cause of the Lord Jesus Christ.

We need a context in which to evaluate this emphasis upon celebrities and personalities, because it is not a phenomenon confined to evangelicalism. In fact, an emphasis on personalities pervades Western society, and our fascination with them is another illustration of the spirit of the age invading the church. James MacGregor Burns, in his perceptive book, *Leadership*, has effectively characterized this climate of the times:

One of the universal cravings of our time is a hunger for compelling and creative leadership. Many of us spent our early years in the eras of the titans—Freud and Einstein, Shaw and Stravinsky, Mao and Gandhi, Churchill and Roosevelt, Stalin and Hitler and Mussolini. Most of these colossi died in the middle years of this century; some lingered on, while a few others—de Gaulle, Nehru, perhaps Kennedy and King— joined the pantheon of leadership. These giants strode across our cultural and intellectual and political horizons. We—followers everywhere—loved or loathed them. We marched for them and fought against them. We died for them and we killed some of them. We could not ignore them.

In the final quarter of our century that life-and-death engagement with leadership has given way to the cult of personality, to a "gee whiz" approach to celebrities. We peer into the private lives of leaders, as though their sleeping habits, eating preferences, sexual practices, dogs, and hobbies carry messages of profound significance. Entire magazines are devoted to trivia about "people," and serious newspapers start off their news stories with a personality ancedote or slant before coming to the essence of the matter. Huge throngs parade in Red Square and in the T'ien An Men Square with giant portraits of men who are not giants. The personality cult—a cult of devils as well as heroes—thrives in both East and West.[1]

When this fascination is brought into the church, the results are both bizarre and damaging. On a recent Christian television program, a man announced, "We're starting a new church. It's a fundamental, soul-winning, Bible-believing church, and this Sunday our special guest star is . . ." Special guest star? What is this? Some churches are now paying $5,000 to $10,000 a night for Christian superstars to appear at their services. One midwestern Baptist church has a Christian Hall of Fame, and in the foyer of their church they have pictures of the ten current best Christians. One prayer-meeting year was promoted by a national advertising campaign listing the forty-eight Christian stars with whom you could pray if you attended the conference. And on and on it goes.

But the problem goes beyond the fact that we are elevating the wrong people. We are also looking to them for the wrong reasons. What most of them are emphasizing is their own personal experience. This is hardly surprising since it is all they basically know. But the profound danger here is that the more fantastic or bizarre the experience, the more invitations a person receives to tell his story, the more books he sells, and the more opportunities he has to put himself forward as a spokesman for Christianity. A steady diet of these sensational attention-getting testimonies produces the impression that being spiritual is equated with having visions, revelations, and ecstatic encounters. It perpetuates a craving for unusual experiences that can hold an audience spellbound, and it creates a little or no hunger for Scriptural knowledge and real spiritual depth. A related problem is the subtle glorification of sin. In a desire to magnify the grace of God, the convert often describes at great length and with explicit detail the life of sin from which he was rescued. More than once I have listened to accounts that seemed to do more to portray the glamour of sin or the grand achievements of the celebrity than to promote the glory of Christ. This is a far cry from the attitude a true believer must have toward the old life, "the things of which you are now ashamed," as Paul says (Romans 6:21). This sense of shame is hard to communicate when the life of sin is described in vivid technicolor. The godly life sounds dull in contrast, and the believer whose walk with the Lord Jesus has kept him from gross sin begins to feel like a second-class citizen.

Something is terribly wrong with this superstar mentality we've developed. Christianity was never meant to be a constant parade of celebrity favorites. It was not meant to find its fundamental meaning in each person's private spiritual experience. Let's consider the unhealthy results this "Hollywood Christianity" is producing in the church today.

Three Problem Areas

First, we need to think seriously about what happens to a new Christian athlete, politician, or entertainment celebrity who finds himself in the Christian limelight. His life becomes a frenzy of dashing from one appearance to another, with little time for his conversion experience to take root and to ripen into a growing, maturing walk with the Lord Jesus. It is relatively easy to pick up some current Christian jargon, which has the sound of spirituality, to develop a dramatic account of one's conversion, and to set off on the testimony trail. But there is no opportunity for solid Bible teaching or for genuine long-term fellowship with believers. There is no accountability to believers who will not put you on a pedestal and who will challenge inconsistency or sin in your life. There is an enormous tendency to spiritual pride, as others defer to your opinions in areas about which you know little or nothing, and you are treated as an instant spiritual expert. And when the crunch of temptation or difficult circumstances comes, the "celebrity Christian" often discovers that he has been living in a prolonged state of spiritual infancy so that he lacks the inner resources to handle the pressures. His testimony is polished, but the flow of conversion has worn off and nothing new is flowing in to replace it.

Exploitation is a hard word, but there is no other word to describe how the Christian world uses some of these people. Fifteen years ago the church took all the converted movie stars and set them up as great propagators of the Christian faith. I had a friend who was used that way. He was publicized and ballyhooed, made a public speaker, promoted as a famous Christian, invited all over the country, and kept spinning in a religious rat cage until, sadly, his life went right down the drain. He fell into sin and drifted away from the Lord. He was about forty years old when he came to our church for the first time. He brought his family and they attended regularly to study the Word of God. Only a year later, as he lay in the hospital dying of cancer, he said to me, "John, it's terrible what happened in my life. They ruined my life by exploiting my testimony because I was somebody known. Only in the last year has my life been meaningful."

What a tragedy! The church has got to stop and consider what we're doing to these new Christians by putting them in the spotlight of the Christian superstar world.

One pro football player was approached *within a week of his conversion* by a group of businessmen who offered to pay all his expenses and his salary if he would go into full-time evangelism! He wasn't even sure of John 3:16 and here were Christians wanting to use him! Don Moomaw, a three time All-American linebacker at UCLA in the 1950's and now a Presbyterian minister, speaks of the wounds he still feels over the way he was exploited:

> I've never had an athlete in the pulpit. I have scars all over from people inviting me, saying, 'We want you to come because we know you can get a crowd! And they'll be frank to say that. . . . When people call wanting an athlete to speak in their church, I'll ask, 'Do you want an athlete who may not be able to say very much but who may be a star athlete? Or do you want one who can say something but who may not be a star?' Very often they can't answer that.[2]

Three things accompany this exploitation of Christian celebrities. The first is *immaturity.* The great need for constant growth can only be met when a new Christian, whatever his status, is integrated into a body of believers, where he will be treated as an ordinary believer. A pedestal is not a good environment for growth. The second is *inflation,* a great tendency to pride. The warning of Paul is very much to the point when he writes that a church leader should not be "a new convert, lest he become conceited and fall into the condemnation incurred by the devil" (1 Timothy 3:6). Granted that these people are not serving as elders, but the wisdom of the principle is apparent. The third concern is *inconsistency.* Many of these baby Christians are living a life radically inconsistent with the message they are proclaiming. This is not surprising, since they are just baby Christians, learning to take their baby steps. Often many areas of their lives need to be brought into conformity with the lordship of Christ. What glory is brought to Christ when a person engaged in making obscene movies or continuing a career as a sensuous rock singer or an athlete living an openly promiscuous life breathlessly tells us of new life in Christ? When the church allows such people to become semiofficial spokesmen, it is certainly giving forth a very uncertain sound!

Secondly, let's think about what the non-Christian sees in the world of Christian super saints, celebrities, and personal experience. Are non-Christians seeing the gospel and the Christian community that Jesus said should be salt to the earth as they observe this celebrity fascination? How do they respond when the gospel is marketed with the same kind of celebrity endorsements a soap manufacturer uses?

Listen to one perceptive unbeliever. In a *New Times* article of September 3, 1976, Larry King wrote:

> I'm not real big on the Jesus movement, a peculiarity which apparently puts me out of the cultural mainstream these days. The Jesus business is no longer confined to the fruit jar whiskey backwoods. You cannot walk through Washington Square Park in Greenwich Village without trembling bug-eyed prophets laying a lot of syrupy sweet Jesus rhetoric on you. Most of them have no foggy notion of what they are talking about. I'm an old Biblical student raised among foot-washing Baptists and I'm simply appalled at how few of the Jesus folk who solicit me are conversant with the Holy Scriptures. Nor are they informed as to the history of religions, Christian or otherwise. Mention the Holy Wars or beg information on how the King James Version of the Bible won out over its rivals and all you get is a blank look and the blanket assurance that Jesus loves you. No, my complaint is not against Jesus but against those who misuse the notion of Him. I have had my fill of high school football coaches praying in His name for victory, of Lions Clubs soliciting Him to bless their annual broom sale, of John Birchers beseeching Him to keep a wary eye on the North Koreans and of white-collar criminals who claim their conversion when prison gates loom in their futures. It would be my modest suggestion that perhaps a working Jesus as well as His supervising daddy might be better occupied in sorting out larger injustices and really doesn't need the babel of selfish prayers. I don't pretend to know whether Jesus might have wished it so, but personally I think He's got more class than many of His agents.

Mr. King's cynicism is self-evident and some of his comments are obviously unfair. And yet his analysis has more than a measure of truth. He has received a grotesque picture of the gospel and true Biblical Christianity, because believers have been unequipped "to make a defense to every one who asks you to give an account for the hope that is in you, yet with gentleness and reverence" (1 Peter 3:15). A great deal of blame for this inability is due to the emphasis on the spectacular and the sensational which puts a premium on impressive performances, at the expense of consistent disciple-making. Unfortunately, the non-Christian often sees through this spiritual superficiality much quicker than the church does.

Third, we need to consider how today's superficial spirituality is influencing the church. God intended for Christians to have examples to follow, truly spiritual leaders who are mature, godly men and women. Thus Paul writes to the Corinthians, "Be imitators of me, just as I also am of Christ" (1 Corinthians 11:1). The problem is not that we have spiritual models but that we have the wrong kind. If we consistently exalt and promote new, immature Christians, we will never have the mature examples we need. Rather, we will perpetuate an emphasis upon personal experience rather than upon the Word of God and, inevitably, we will produce immature, superficial churches and Christians. We will overlook the unspectacular, humble, and gentle believers who have the servant mentality of the Lord Jesus, the very people to whom we ought to look as examples and teachers. Tragically, as the church emphasizes the sensational and the bizarre, it neglects the solid instruction which is essential to produce the growth of baby Christians into mature disciples. If the current trend is not checked, the church will become weaker and weaker (although perhaps larger and larger) until it will have little positive influence on Christians or non-Christians.

Finding The Solution

It is not difficult to diagnose problems, but it is quite another thing to point the way to a solution. At first glance the whole problem may seem to be only a relatively harmless aberration. After all, what permanent damage can be done by emphasizing a new breed of Christian hero, especially when it seems that crowds will come to hear such a person? But a closer examination reveals that some basic and fundamental issues are involved and three need to be considered in depth.

The Issue of Evangelism

One pressing concern relates to what it means to bear witness to the gospel of the Lord Jesus. If our object is to bring people to the Lord Jesus, what methods should be used to accomplish this goal? If celebrities further the cause of fulfilling the Great Commission, why not seek as many endorsements from as many sources as possible? If people who are opinion makers within the world's framework can be mobilized to testify to the work of Jesus Christ, who can be less than thankful?

We are profoundly grateful to God for every true proclamation of the gospel of the Lord Jesus Christ. But there are some basic Biblical truths about evangelism that must not be ignored. We live in a time when the term "born-again Christian" has entered the cultural mainstream, but the fact that a term is widely used does not mean that it is widely understood. Furthermore, there is a bewildering abundance of evangelistic programs and organizations, but there is often a great ignorance of our responsibility as ambassadors of the Lord Jesus Christ. The Word of God not only tells us what we are to proclaim, but how we are to proclaim it:

> Therefore, since we have this ministry, as we received mercy, we do not lose heart, but we have renounced the things hidden because of shame, not walking in craftiness or adulterating the word of God, but by the manifestation of truth commending ourselves to every man's conscience in the sight of God. And even if our gospel is veiled, it is veiled to those who are perishing, in whose case the god of this world has blinded the minds of the unbelieving, that they might not see the light of the gospel of the glory of Christ, who is the image of God. For we do not preach ourselves but Christ Jesus as Lord, and ourselves as your bond-servants for Jesus' sake. For God, who said, "Light shall shine out of darkness," is the One who has shone in our hearts to give the light of the knowledge of the glory of God in the face of Christ. But we have this treasure in earthen vessels, that the surpassing greatness of the power may be of God and not from ourselves.
>
> (2 Corinthians 4:1-7)

There are at least four principles of Biblical evangelism given to us in these verses, which must control all that we do in the Lord's name. First of all, *our message must not be man-centered, but Christ-centered.* "We do not preach ourselves but Christ Jesus as Lord," was Paul's basic operating procedure. Our focus must never be on who we are, but on who He is, and what He will do for anyone who comes to Him in faith and trust. Not one single particle is added to the glory of the Lord Jesus by the conversion of the most illustrious person on earth. He is Lord! All the glory in Heaven is His by sovereign right, and our responsibility is to point men to Him alone. We do no favor to the Lord Jesus by emphasizing the worldly credentials of His messengers and subtly shifting the person of our Lord Jesus to a second position. It is not the recounting of the experiences of famous people that saves sinners, it is the simple message of the free grace of God in Jesus Christ. It was not for nothing that Paul said to the Corinthians (to whom personalities were so important), "I determined to know nothing among you except Jesus Christ, and Him crucified" (1 Corinthians 2:2).

A second principle given to us by Paul is that, in our evangelism, *we must reject manipulative methods*. We have renounced hidden devices and crafty methods. The word "craftiness" used in verse two literally means a willingness to do anything to gain a desired goal. It is the old philosophy that "the end justifies the means." Paul is concerned to tell us that our methods must have a godly integrity that rejects manipulation. This is extremely relevant to our subject because an emphasis on "celebrityism" or sensational experiences can easily be manipulative. It tells people that faith in Christ can be a route to "health and wealth," or it stirs our emotions to seek similar experiences, without engaging our minds. "Trust Christ so you can become like Joe Superstar or Jane Bombshell." We need to be very careful here. This is the technique of the Madison Avenue huckster or the political propagandist. But the gospel is not a bandwagon we ride on, it is a Person we trust.

Ray Stedman, in a study of the way Satan seduced Eve into sin, points out that Satan's technique was to move Eve to a decision on the basis of her emotions and senses, carefully disengaging her mind from the decision-making process. He then goes on to give a very helpful analysis of our responsibility in evangelism:

> In man as God made him, the order is to be, first, an appeal to the mind, then the stirring of the emotions based upon the facts presented to the mind; and then the two working together, the mind and emotions, to move the will. This is why, throughout the Scriptures, the appeal of the gospel, the good news from God, is addressed first to the mind.
>
> That is why any evangelism which does not begin with teaching is a false evangelism. Any evangelism which moves directly to an appeal to the will to act, or to the emotions to feel, is distorted and results in abortion instead of birth.[3]

Closely related to the rejection of a manipulative method is the third principle Paul gives us. *Our evangelism must not proclaim a manipulated message*, for we are not "adulterating the word of

God." The word "adulterate" refers to the practice of mixing God's Word with popular philosophies to make it more suitable to a mass market. It is a danger far more real than we care to admit, and especially if the proclamation of the gospel is continually entrusted into the hands of the spiritually immature. There is a great temptation to make it less difficult and more popular, but, in the process, the gospel is actually falsified. Many of the current presentations of the gospel bear little resemblance to the message the New Testament thunders forth. James Denney, the Scottish theologian, speaks of going fishing with a friend who felt a strike on his line. But when he pulled in his line, he discovered the barb had broken off the hook, so that the fish had escaped with the bait. From that incident, he draws a profound truth:

> The condemnation of our sins in Christ upon His cross is the barb on the hook. If you leave that out of your Gospel, I do not deny that your bait will be taken, but you will not catch men. You will not create in human hearts that attitude to Christ which created the New Testament. You will not annihilate pride, and make Christ the Alpha and Omega in man's redemption.[4]

The fourth evangelistic principle of importance in 2 Corinthians 4 is that *effectiveness is due not to the adequacy of the messenger but to the power of God.* God does not need great men and famous celebrities to promote His cause. "We have this treasure in earthen vessels, that the surpassing greatness of the power may be of God and not from ourselves." Both Biblical and church history reinforce this principle. God delights to take people whom the world would overlook and accomplish great things through them. No one illustrates this more clearly than Paul. Within Judaism, he was a celebrity, the up-and-coming theologian of his day, the Pharisee of the Pharisees. His conversion experience was sensational within Hebrew society. But God's Word to Paul was, "Go! For I will send you far away to the Gentiles" (Acts 22:21). That was an area where Paul was no celebrity and had little experience, but God made him tremendously effective, because Paul learned that his adequacy was not of himself but of God (2 Corinthians 3:5, 6). This is not to say that God will never use a celebrity in a significant way, but it is to say that He will not use a person just because he is a celebrity. James Denney has a significant word:

> There have always been men in the world so clever that God could make no use of them; they could never do His work because they were

so lost in admiration of their own. But God's work never depended on them and it does not depend on them now. It depends on those who, when they see Jesus Christ, become unconscious, once and forever, of all that they had been used to call their wisdom and their strength . . . The kingdom of God has not changed its administration since the first century; its supreme law is still the glory of God and not the glory of the clever man; and we may be sure that it will not change. God will always have His work done by instruments who are willing to have it clear that the exceeding greatness of the power is His, and not theirs.[5]

It is precisely this law that our obsession with personalities violates. Until we realize that God and His Word, not man and his works, are the basis of all true evangelism, we will continue to abound in superficial spirituality.

The Issue of Authority

November 1978 is a date to be etched in the memory. In the shocking mass suicide in a jungle in Guyana, the personality cult reached its grotesque climax. Jm Jones and Jonestown bears gory witness to the tragedy that ensues when authority is invested in impressive personalities or in spectacular experiences, rather than in the written Word of God. Years before the Jonestown tragedy, a young friend was invited to a meeting at which Jim Jones was the speaker. Those who attended were asked to register their names, addresses, and phone numbers at the door. A few minutes later, as later investigation showed, my friend's mother received a phone call from a woman claiming to be a real estate agent who was curiously interested in some details about the home and the family. Later in the meeting, Jim Jones claimed he had a revelation from God about my friend, and he called her to stand. When he then recounted some details he, as a total stranger, could never have known (and which his accomplice had passed along), my friend was both terrified and awestruck. Humanly speaking, only a mother who was committed to the absolute authority of the Word of God, and who was spiritually sensitive, saved my friend from being swept away in Jim Jones' personality cult.

Jim Jones is dead and gone, but his legacy is far more alive than we care to admit. The issue of final authority is a burning one in evangelical circles, and it directly involves us in the question of truth. Is truth to be discerned in the number of famous people who endorse a claim or movement? Is truth to be found in the unverifiable experiences of professing Christians? Does authority lie in the powerful, persuasive, confident leader who majors on the spectacular and the impressive? Or does it lie in the written Word of God which is "inspired by God and profitable for teaching, for reproof, for correction, for training in righteousness, that the man of God may be adequate, equipped for every good work" (2 Timothy 3:16, 17). Surely to ask that question is to answer it. It is not the words of men but the Word of God that is "the sword of the Spirit" (Ephesians 6:17), "living and active and sharper than any two-edged sword, and piercing as far as the division of soul and spirit, of both joints and marrow, and able to judge the thoughts and intentions of the heart" (Hebrews 4:12). It is Scripture that is more to be desired than much fine gold (Psalm 119:10), that "will make your way prosperous" (Joshua 1:8), keep us from sin (Psalm 119:11), and enable us to be "approved to God as a workman" (2 Timothy 2:15). So important is the Word of God that the Lord Jesus says, "If you abide in My word, then you are truly disciples of Mine" (John 8:31).

It is not enough to give lip service to the authority of Scripture. The most urgent need of believers is to know, understand, apply, and obey the Word of God. But when we are faced with a constant stream of subjective experiences and personal impressions from even the most well-meaning Christian, we will inevitably produce immaturity and superficiality. When quality time is given over to the telling and hearing of exciting stories, it is no wonder that our churches grow fat but they do not grow strong. No one involved in working with Christians can fail to be heartbroken at the massive ignorance of the Word of God modern evangelicalism displays. Emotionalism wears very thin under the grinding pressures of life, and Christians who lack a solid foundation in the Word of God all too soon become brittle and broken. How we need to hear Paul's word, "Preach the word; be ready in season and out of season; reprove, rebuke, exhort, with great patience and instruction" (2 Timothy 4:2). The old axiom, "The good is often the enemy of the best," surely applies here. Testimonies, experiences, sharing—all these are well and good at times. But when they become a staple in our spiritual diet, we are gorging ourselves on spiritual junk food.

Related to this issue of the authority of Scripture is the position a Christian leader is to take in relation to it. He is to be a servant, consumed with the desire to elevate the Lord Jesus. Andrew

Bonar, from a sickbed, recorded these words in his diary: "Today missed some fine opportunities of speaking a word for Christ. The Lord saw that I would have spoken as much as for my own honor as His, and therefore, He shut my mouth. *I see a man cannot be a faithful servant until he preaches Christ for Christ's sake—until* he gives up striving to attract people to himself and seeks only to attract them to Christ. Lord, give me this!"

Every Christian leader must fight the pernicious tendency to take for ourselves a glory that belongs to the Lord Jesus. We delight in recounting a man's achievements and applauding his fine qualities, and in the process we subtly place him on a pedestal beyond contradiction or accountability. Our Christian world is full of demanding, domineering leaders who have forgotten the principle the Lord so clearly put forth in Luke 22:25-27:

> And He said to them: "The kings of the Gentiles lord it over them; and those who have authority over them are called 'Benefactors.' But not so with you, but let him who is the greatest among you become as the youngest, and the leader as the servant. For who is greater, the one who reclines at table, or the one who serves? Is it not the one who reclines at table? But I am among you as the one who serves."

Our emphasis on personalities and celebrities does far more to produce a generation of Christian recliners and spectators than it does a corps of humble servants, committed to pay any price for the privilege of serving the Lord Jesus Christ. The only authority in the church is His authority as its risen head, and nothing that takes place in His church must diminish His authority.

The Issue of True Spirituality

The nature of true spirituality seems to have gotten lost behind the smoke screen of glamor and sensationalism. But the crucial question remains: What does it really mean to be spiritual? Each person offering his own opinion simply adds to the frenzy of confusion since one person's opinion is no more valid than another's. But God in His wisdom has given us a standard by which to measure each private opinion. God's Word, the Bible, lays down the guidelines to lead us through the confusion and to show us clearly the path to true spirituality, and like most other truths revealed by our great and marvelous God, the path is very different from what we might expect.

True spirituality, according to the Bible, is Christlike character. The goal is character, not who can have more visions than anyone else. This character is described in Galatians 5:22, 23: "The fruit of the Spirit is love, joy, peace, gentleness, goodness, faith, humility and self-control." This is the character sketch of the person God's Spirit is molding us to be. Maturity—spirituality—is nothing less than Christlike character. Now if this is the ultimate goal, how do we get there? Which direction do we take through the maze? Are there several directions, one just as good as another? Or is there only one right path clearly laid out by the Father?

The Bible teaches that walking in the Spirit, that is, living daily in the power of the Holy Spirit, is the road we must all travel if we want to be truly spiritual. Mysterious as this sounds to some believers, it actually involves two simple steps: receiving the Word of God and living it out in obedience. In 1 Corinthians 3, Paul said to the Corinthian Christians: "I could not speak unto you as unto spiritual, but as unto carnal." Why were they carnal? "I gave you milk to drink, not solid food; for you were not yet able to receive it. Indeed, even now you are not yet able, for you are still fleshly. For since there is jealousy and strife among you, are you not fleshly, and are you not walking like mere men?" (1 Corinthians 3:1-3). In the Corinthian church the believers were not able to receive the Word or to obey it, and as a result, they continued to be carnal, not spiritual.

The Road to Revival

In the midst of all our modern superstar Christianity, many people are proclaiming revival. Because so many people are talking about God, Christians assume this must be what spirituality and revival are like—a widespread interest in "Christian" things and many claims to be "born again." But, according to Scripture, these are not the evidence of true revival. That requires far more than crowds of people dashing about announcing that "Jesus is a groovy trip."

Psalm 85 establishes the two elements of true revival. The plea for revival in the first seven verses says in part: "Wilt Thou be angry with us forever? Wilt Thou prolong Thine anger to all generations? Wilt Thou not Thyself revive us again, That Thy people may rejoice in Thee?" The Israelites had been chastened by God, and thus had spent long years in exile in Babylon. Now, at last, they cried out for spiritual revival. In verse 11 the psalmist praises the two elements that always accompany true revival: "Truth shall spring out of the earth; and righteousness shall look down from heaven." Truth and righteousness always accompany the work of the Spirit. True doctrine and right living! This is exactly what Paul was telling the Corinthian church they lacked. They were not spiritual because they had no real commitment to the truth of God in His Word, and they were not able to live righteously by obeying that Word. True spirituality and true revival are always demonstrated in these two ways.

Let's look first at righteousness or right living. In Ezekiel 36:27, the Scriptures say: "And I will put My Spirit within you and cause you to walk in My statutes, and you will be careful to observe My ordinances." The result of the true work of the Spirit then is not visions and ecstasies and special experiences, but rather it is the obedience of righteousness. It is walking in God's truth, keeping His ordinances and doing them.

This obedience of righteousness is two-sided, having both a positive element and a negative element. The positive side is the pursuit of the commandments of God, and the negative side is shown in verse 31 of the passage we just examined: "Then shall ye remember your own evil ways, and your doings that were not good, and shall loathe yourselves in your own sight for your iniquities and for your abominations." If we are truly pursuing righteousness, we will loathe, despise, and hate our own sinfulness. We will have a deep sense of conviction about our sin.

But where is the grief over sin in the modern Christian superstar movement and our so-called current revival? We see a great deal of laughter and frivolity, but there seems to be very little evidence of a deep-burning conviction of sin. Scripture says that if we pursue righteousness and seek to obey God moment by moment, we will often experience deep sorrow as the stench of immorality and self-centeredness fills our nostrils. Sadly, what we see in our country today is not true revival. We hear many believers speaking about God, but we don't see very many weeping over sin and carnality, as the Lord Jesus wept over Jerusalem. We don't see people beating their breasts and crying out in grief over their sin as the people of Nineveh did when Jonah preached and the Spirit of God brought true revival. Righteousness and revival are inseparable.

The second element of true Holy Spirit revival is truth. When revival comes, there will be a deep commitment to divine truth.

The revival in Nehemiah's day began when Nehemiah says, "Bring me the book." As Ezra the priest read from the book, which was the law of Moses, and explained its meaning, the people began to mourn and weep because of their failure to keep the law. The beginning of their revival meant spending days listening to the reading and explanation of the Word, so that they might confess their sins, repent, and begin to live righteous lives. Biblical exposition and instruction are the work of the Spirit. Through knowledge and understanding of God's Word, the Holy Spirit produces a deep conviction of sin and a desire for holy living. Such conviction and holy living doesn't result in a Christian elitist group who think they are above the rest of the world and occasionally condescend to them, but a body of believers who are salt and light in the world, walking through the world as Jesus walked, changing men as Jesus did.

The apostle Paul also made definite connection between a commitment to the Word and spirituality. Ephesians 5:18 says, "Be filled with the Spirit," and Colossians 3:16 says, "Let the word of Christ richly dwell within you." An examination of the context in both epistles quickly indicates that these two verses are parallel passages expressing essentially the same meaning in different words. The results are so much the same that one verse could be a substitute for the other, and so we are given the important insight that being "filled with the Spirit" leads to the same results as letting "the word of Christ richly dwell within you." To be Scripture-controlled is to be Spirit-filled.

The Holy Spirit is the "Spirit of truth." So where there is true revival, there is a hunger for, and commitment to, truth, and there is an emphasis on righteous living—not gifts, signs, visions, wonders, revelations, and ecstasies.

Scripture gives many examples of truly spiritual men. In the Old Testament, Isaiah the prophet was allowed to see a vision of God in all His holiness, but Isaiah didn't rush out to announce his personal spiritual experience. Instead, he mourned his own sin and described himself as a man of "unclean lips." In the New Testament, when Peter was confronted with the power of Jesus expressed through an incredible miracle, he fell on his face and said, "Depart from me, for I am a sinful man, O Lord" (Luke 5:8). Just a few verses later, Peter "left everything and followed Christ" (Luke 5:11). He was the kind of man for whom Jesus was looking—a humble man with a deep sense of his own sin.

The early church had no celebrities and no gimmicks. They were simply godly people living in an ungodly society and having a phenomenal influence. In fact, it is important to realize that when the early church did deal with personalities and celebrities, it was in a context of spiritual confusion and doctrinal departure. When the Corinthian church began, at the urging of some false apostles, to question Paul's position of authority and leadership over them, they themselves claimed some impressive personal and experiential qualifications. In response, what credentials did Paul present to defend his spirituality and right to leadership? In 2 Corinthians 12:1-10, Paul describes his own vision and personal spiritual experience, and it is instructive to see how he deals with it. This was an experience that would have captured the imagination of modern Christians—a personal expedition to the third heaven, and a vision of glory that defied human language! In fact we are plagued with a rash of books and articles claiming to have experienced this kind of "out of body" experience. Sadly, many Christians show more excitement about these claims than they do for the plain teaching of God's Word. Paul's attitude is very different. He is very reluctant to speak about the experience, clearly indicates that it was exceptional rather than normal, since it had occurred fourteen years earlier, and emphasizes that God had drawn a veil of silence across the incident. In fact, the Lord had driven a stake into his flesh (the familiar word "thorn" in verse seven is far weaker than the Greek word), to keep him from pride over the event.

But Paul was not without credentials. The marks of reality in his life were not marks of power and great personal achievement, but the supernatural evidence of the work of the Holy Spirit and God's grace in the midst of Paul's weaknesses and infirmities. Seen in that light, 2 Corinthians 11:23-29 gives us a remarkable insight into the Biblical view of spirituality, a concept that bears little resemblance to a smooth, sophisticated tinsel-town spirituality. Speaking of the false apostles who were harassing the Corinthians, Paul writes:

Are they servants of Christ? (I speak as if insane) I more so; in far more labors, in far more imprisonments, beaten times without number, often in danger of death. Five times I received from the Jews thirty-nine lashes. Three times I was beaten with rods, once I was stoned, three times I was shipwrecked, a night and a day I have spent in the deep. I have been on frequent journeys, in dangers from rivers, dangers from robbers, dangers from my countrymen, dangers from the Gentiles, dangers in the city, dangers in the wilderness, dangers on the sea, dangers among false brethren; I have been in labor and hardship, through many sleepless nights, in hunger and thirst, often without food, in cold and exposure. Apart from such external things, there is the daily pressure upon me of concern for all the churches. Who is weak without my being weak? Who is led into sin without my intense concern?

Here are the real evidences of Paul's spirituality. His commitment to teach God's truth and his overwhelming desire to be obedient to God's will resulted in a life of affliction and persecution. He wasn't laughing and joking all the time, and he wasn't sitting around boasting about how spiritual he was because he had had visions and revelations from God. Most of the time, he was running for his life!

Finally, we need to consider the example of our Lord Jesus himself. His life was also one of suffering and humiliation. He wept over the destruction that sin was causing. He struggled in agony against the temptations of Satan. He was beaten, publicly humiliated, and executed as a criminal. Of course, there was a deep inner joy in fellowship with the Father and in doing the Father's will, but there was also pain and great sorrow.

In Matthew 5, Jesus talks about the kind of joy and happiness that true spirituality brings: "Blessed (happy) are the poor in spirit . . . (happy) are those who mourn . . . (happy) are the gentle . . . (happy) are those who hunger and thirst for righteousness . . . (happy) are the merciful . . . (happy) are the pure in heart . . . (happy) are the peacemakers . . . (happy) are those who have been persecuted for the sake of righteousness . . . (happy) are you when men revile you, and persecute you, and say all kinds of evil against you falsely, on account of Me. Rejoice, and be glad, for your reward in heaven is great, for so they persecuted the prophets who were before you." Are the really happy people the ones who laugh and joke all the time? No, happy people are humble Christians who experience persecution as they struggle to live righteously in an ungodly society.

What are Christians seeking today as their goal? Is it purity of life, or is it freedom from earthly troubles? We often hear that the Holy Spirit will cure all ills and smooth all the rough bumps along the road of life. He will heal you of any disease, and He will remove every problem. The Holy Spirit is portrayed as offering to all Christians a candy-coated life with no bitter taste. But mature believers don't look for the candy-coated life; they confess with David in Psalm 119:71: "It is good for me that I was afflicted."

We will not all suffer as Jesus and Paul did, but we must get our goals and our values straightened out. According to the Bible, our goal should be holy living in accordance with God's truth as revealed in His Word. Any lesser goal will not produce true spirituality.

The church today is facing a great danger in this area. If we continue to settle for counterfeit spirituality, we are going to lose sight of the real thing. Let's stop exalting people who are not truly spiritual. Paul makes it clear in his instructions in 1 Timothy that new converts should not be given positions of leadership and responsibility—they should first demonstrate maturity through righteous living and knowledge of God's Word. Let's make true spirituality our goal and begin to exalt mature Christians who are humble and manifest the character of Christ, those who can teach us God's Word and teach us to live righteous lives. Let's choose Christians whose lives demonstrate grief over sin and a hunger for holiness. Together let's become a church which is characterized by true spirituality.

Robert Murray McCheyne, that godly Scot of the last century, lived a short life that left a long impact for the Lord. He once wrote some words to a friend studying for the ministry, which bear repeating a century later:

> I trust you will have a pleasant and profitable time in Germany. I know you will apply hard to German, but do not forget the culture of the inner man. I mean of the heart. How diligently the cavalry officer keeps his sabre clean and sharp, every stain he rubs off with the greatest care. Remember, you are God's sword—His instrument—I trust a chosen vessel unto Him to bear His name. In great measure, according to the purity and perfections of the instrument will be the success. *It is not great talents God blesses so much as great likeness to Jesus.* A holy Christian is an awesome weapon in the hand of God.

How much we need to hear that truth!

---

³Ray C. Stedman, *Understanding Man* (Waco, Texas: Word Books, 1975), pp. 75,76.

⁴James Denney, *Studies in Theology* (London: Hodder and Stoughton, 1895), pp. 127, 128.

⁵James Denney, "The Second Epistle to the Corinthians," in W. Robertson Nicoll, editor, *The Expositor's Bible* (New York: A. C. Armstrong and Son, 1894), p. 160.

THE NATION

Whatever Became of the Pilgrim/Puritan Dream?

by LeRoy Lawson

America remains the world's most successful experiment in democracy. No other constitutional democracy has guaranteed the right to vote to so many of its citizens for so long a time. No other has suffered such threats to its stability as our war between the states and the Watergate scandal and emerged without anarchy or tyranny. What other nation has responded so rapidly to the changing demands of its constituents or managed so successfully to distribute its wealth on such a broad basis without curtailing basic freedoms or imposing crippling governmental controls? America has consistently been able to boast of freedoms other nations have only dreamed about.

The list of America's virtues could be lengthened, but enough has been said to establish that we Americans have many reasons for appreciating our heritage. Yet the purpose of this essay is not to offer a litany of praise but to lament the loss of three essentials of democracy. It is apparent that something has changed our society in the twentieth century. A quick review of newspaper headlines—or, more importantly, of judicial decisions by our Supreme and lesser courts—reveals that the vision of America's founding fathers has faded. Three guiding essentials that informed the decisions of our earliest Pilgrim and Puritan colonists and that powerfully influenced the framers of our Constitution are no longer dominant forces in our democracy. These three fundamentals are the pioneers' concern for posterity, their profound humility, and their sense of mission. The concern for posterity has yielded to an hedonistic preoccupation with the present; the loss of humility before God, man, and Scripture has led to an arrogant faith in the supremacy of man; and the loss of a sense of mission has left us with maintenance ideals and placed us on the defensive in the world community. Each of these losses deserves further examination.

From Vision to Daydream

The distance America has traveled from the values of our colonial forefathers to those of contemporary society is the difference between living for posterity and preoccupation with the present. It is not easy for the Now Generation, which demands instant gratification of every whim, devours magazines like *Us* and *Self* and books like *Winning Through Intimidation* and *Looking Out for Number One*, and burns natural resources with scarcely a thought about the future, to comprehend the sacrificial spirit of the country's founders. To them nothing mattered so much as making a better world for their children and grandchildren. When Thomas Paine pleaded for the war of independence, he gave voice to the yearning that had been in the hearts of America's leaders from the founding of the little colony at Plymouth Rock: " 'Tis not the concern of a day, a year, or an age; posterity are virtually involved in the contest and will be . . . affected by it to the end of time.'' On the day John Adams signed the Declaration of Independence, he wrote Abigail, ''Through all the gloom I can see the rays of ravishing light and glory. Posterity will triumph in that day's transaction.'' At the close of his life, Thomas Jefferson wrote to his old comrade-in-arms, President James Madison, ''It has been a great solace to me to believe that you are engaged in vindicating to posterity the course we have pursued, of preserving to them, in all their purity, the blessings of self-government which we had assisted in acquiring for them.''

Wherever one turns in the early generations of America's history, he finds this concern for the country's future. The earliest European arrivals on the continent believed themselves to be charting a new course. Their God had led them to their promised land, to found a Christian civilization in the wilderness. They would have to struggle and sacrifice, but their children would experience what they could only envision. Their vision was of a future vastly different from their beleaguered past. For them the new world meant rebirth. Not everyone had the same dream, of course. There were among them selfless Christians with a desire to do God's bidding above everything else. There were also the poor, with visions of riches dancing in their heads; there were the sick seeking health, the weak dreaming of strength, the intimidated hoping for new confidence and freedom. Freedom—that is what they all wanted. If they themselves could not have it to the fullest, they wanted to guarantee that their children would. They knew how to wait, to do without, to sacrifice, for the sake of their posterity.

We hear precious little about our children's world these days. In spite of the warnings of futurologists, Americans continue to plunder the resources of land and water, to spew poisons into their air, to play insane games of international brinksmanship, and to pile up gargantuan national debts, borrowing from the future for today's pleasure. The ethic of self-denial is heard only in the pitifully weak voices of the concerned few. When Archie Bunker asserts that "there's three great things that happens to a man in his lifetime. Buying a house . . . a car . . . and a new color TV. That's what America is all about," he verbalizes the ethic of the Now Generation. It is consumerism gone wild, demanding and enjoying constitutional rights but not giving even lip service to corresponding responsibilities.

This is not to propose that *all* pioneers were more concerned about posterity than about themselves, nor that all of today's Americans subscribe to a pleasure ethic. Reinhold Niebuhr is undoubtedly right in noting that a dichotomy has always existed in America's history. Ours is a "religious" nation, if we mean by that term that religious organizations enjoy a larger membership and a more devoted loyalty than any other nation of the Western world; it is "secular," on the other hand, in our unquestioning pursuit of the immediate goals of life without regard to the ultimate questions of meaning. But when one reads through the documents of our earliest history, he is impressed that the ultimate questions were indeed being asked then, and that in spite of the settlers' necessary attention to such immediate goals as food and shelter, their descendants' devotion to pleasure and self-fulfillment *now* would have come as a shock to the God-fearing pioneers.

It came as a shock to one of our contemporaries. In 1978 the famed Russian novelist Alexander Solzhenitsyn, who has found political asylum in America, gave his first major speech in three years at Harvard's commencement. We Americans gloated when this refugee from Communist repression took shelter among us, congratulating ourselves upon our propaganda victory, and commending him for having the good judgment to flee to us. But some of the newspapers which greeted him so warmly soon published their resentment of the latter-day prophet's moral preachments. In his Harvard address he attacked American society on many issues: civic cowardice, immoral legalism, licentious journalism, America's capitulation in Asia, and our godless humanism. He could testify from experience, "that a society without any objective legal scale is a terrible one indeed," but he added that "a society with no other scale but the legal one is not quite worthy of man either."

Solzhenitsyn had observed Americans' compulsive habit of running to the courts to settle disputes. The cry for rights— women's rights, racial rights, children's rights, unborn children's rights, mothers' rights of life and death over unborn children, rights to privacy, rights to guaranteed income—has not impressed him. He could not hold the West up as a model to his Communist homeland. He found that Russia's intense suffering had developed a spirituality that makes the decadent West quite unattractive by comparison. "After the suffering of decades of violence and oppression, the human soul longs for things higher, warmer, and purer than those offered by today's mass living habits."

Not content simply to catalogue our faults, Solzhenitsyn seeks the cause of the West's defection. At the root is an erroneous world view, he says, one he defines as "rationalistic humanism . . . the proclaimed and enforced autonomy of man from any higher force above him." Because we do not worship God, we do obeisance to man and his material desires.

It was not so in the beginning. With American and other democracies, "All individual human rights were granted because man is God's creature. That is, freedom was given to the individual conditionally, in the assumption of his constant religious responsibility." When the West discarded her reliance upon God, "a total liberation occurred from the moral heritage of Christian centuries with their great reserves of mercy and sacrifice."

What then is left? A country that was founded by God-fearers who believed themselves to be establishing a nation on divine principles has given way to a prosperous, materialistic people who have themselves become the measure of all things and who look to no inspired guide. Two forces, democracy and Christianity, have been partners throughout most of our history. Now they are painfully separated and headed toward divorce. Every year the court calendars are crowded with litigation as yet another group sues to protect the populace from God. Every Christmas someone goes to court to ban nativity scenes from courthouses or even the singing of Christmas carols from music curricula in public schools. The nation's values are being ripped from their religious roots. Rudolf the Red-Nosed Reindeer and Santa Claus are acceptable subjects for Christmas music, but not Jesus.

A cartoon several years ago shows Uncle Sam, standing on the Ship of State, addressing representatives of the Christian faith, "It is your business to keep off from the Ship of State the barnacles of greed, selfishness, and dishonesty." That sounds good, and, were even that much being accomplished, posterity would have some hope. But as Solzhenitsyn has pointed out, that's not good enough. Christian representatives must also have something to say about the mission of the ship, lest eventually posterity have no ship to sail.

When foreign policy is decided on the basis of what sells the most grain for American farmers now, and what protects the flow of oil into the country now, and what is best for corporate profits now, greed and the "right" of Americans to prosper in the face of world poverty may lead to a war that will annihilate American democracy. When the welfare state goes further and further into debt, with municipalities and states and the federal government alike allocating huge handouts to the nonworking, and with the birth of generation after generation of welfare babies who will grow up to expect lifetime subsidy, a bankrupt government could lose its future through today's gluttony. The Now Generation cannot be trusted to guard the fortunes of posterity.

From Humility to Arrogance
Everyone knows that the Pilgrim and Puritan settlers of America were religious. What everyone does not know is that even a Deist like Thomas Jefferson believed our national destiny rests with Providence rather than with human power. Jefferson had proposed that the seal of the United States depict this dependence upon God. He wanted it to be a picture of the children of Israel being led by a cloud by day and a pillar of fire by night.

Another Deist, Benjamin Franklin, in a famous speech to the Constitutional Convention June 28, 1787, bemoaning that the small progress the convention had made over several weeks of deliberation was "melancholy Proof of the Imperfection of the Human understanding," chided his colleagues for not having prayed "to the Father of Lights to illuminate our Understandings." He recalled that "in the Beginning of the Contest with Britain, when we were sensible of Danger," they had daily prayed in that same room for divine protection—and that protection was granted. "To that Kind Providence we owe this happy Opportunity of Consulting in Peace on the Means of establishing our future national Felicity." In an almost prophetic rhetorical question, Franklin asked, "And have we now forgotten that powerful Friend—or *do we imagine we no longer need its Assistance?*"

Franklin's question seems pertinent today: Do we no longer need God's assistance?

When the founding fathers wrote as the first amendment, "Congress shall make no law respecting an establishment of religion, or prohibiting the free exercise thereof," they clearly intended to prohibit the development of a European state-church on American soil, but they did not mean to prohibit the free expression of faith. Yet recent court decisions have made the Constitution say something that never was intended. It is apparent that a new religious force has overthrown traditional Christianity in America. The new state religion is Atheism.

The secular prevails; human reason is the arbiter of right and wrong.

While the Constitution correctly prohibits any established religion from being forced upon the citizens of the United States, the Constitution was not designed to separate God from state in the way which we are now allowing in our judiciary system. There is, unfortunately, a bitter truth in the well-publicized cartoon showing two children kneeling in a corridor of a public elementary school. Their teacher, after realizing that the children are using dice to gamble, says with obvious relief, "Thank Goodness! I thought at first you were praying." The cartoon unwittingly demonstrates the unfortunate result of recent judicial decisions.

The earliest founders not only believed in God, but they believed in themselves. Their self-confidence was qualified, however. They subscribed to the paradoxical view of man which orthodox Christianity has always taught: man was created in the image of God and is therefore capable of extraordinary achievements; man is a sinner who has fallen from God's grace and is therefore not to be trusted. Nevertheless, he possesses incredible potential.

That was the opinion of John Preston, an early Puritan preacher: "He is in heauen, and wee are on earth; hee the glorious God, we dust and ashes; hee the Creator, and wee but creatures; and yet he is willing to enter into Couenant, which implyes a kinde of equality betweene vs." Without this faith in man, democracy is impossible. At the same time, Christianity's clear-eyed view of human weakness refuses to grant the democratic majority absolute rule, fearful that human sinfulness will cause the majority to trample upon the rights of the minority. The model is Jesus Christ ("the first true democrat that ever breathed," said James Russell Lowell), who "did not count equality with God a thing to be grasped, but emptied himself, taking the form of a servant ..." (Philippians 2:6, 7, *Revised Standard Version*). "Having all authority in heaven and earth," He did not use His power to tyrannize, but to serve and save.

American democracy has always rested on this Christian view of man, as Reinhold Niebuhr stated so succinctly in our century, "Man's capacity for justice makes democracy possible; but man's inclination to injustice makes democracy necessary." Elton Trueblood modified Niebuhr slightly: "Democracy is necessitated by the fact that all men are sinners; it is made possible by the fact that we know it."

The earliest generations of pioneers would have agreed with Thomas Jefferson's dictum that there is "no safe depository of the ultimate powers of the society but the people themselves," but would have had less confidence than he that "if we think them not enlightened enough to exercise their control with a wholesome discretion, the remedy is not take it from them, but to inform their discretion by education." They would not have taken the power from them, either, and they would also have wanted to inform their discretion by education, but they lacked Jefferson's optimism concerning the ability of education alone to make men worthy of self-rule.

They could have predicted twentieth-century parents' disillusionment with education. Having for so long believed that education could solve all social and political problems, Americans have finally realized that something more fundamental than general knowledge is needed. We can teach information concerning all branches of human science, but without our forefathers' realistic appraisal of the nature of mankind, society will still be in danger. In his farewell address, George Washington, who based his whole argument for constitutional restraint upon the need of "a just estimate of that love of power, and proneness to abuse it, which predominates in the human heart," echoed the colonist's firm conviction. Even Thomas Jefferson, more optimistic about man than the Calvinistic Pilgrims and Puritans, still had to admit practically, "If once the people become inattentive to the public affairs, you and I and Congress and Assemblies, Judges, and Governors, shall all become wolves." Man bears watching. His love of power is dangerous.

They had learned this the hard way. When the Pilgrims arrived here, they were not only seeking to establish a new home; they were also escaping an intolerable monarch. There was certainly no prevailing doctrine in England that all men should be treated equally. In fact, when James I called the state of monarchy "the supremest thing on earth" in his address to Parliament in 1609, he could not have stated the opposite view more clearly:

> Kings are justly called gods, for that they exercise a manner or resemblance of divine power on earth; for if you will consider the attributes of God, you shall see how they agree in the person of a king. God hath power to create or destroy, make or unmake at His pleasure, to give life or send death, to judge all and be judged nor accountable to none . . . And the like power have kings; they make and unmake their subjects, they have power of raising and casting down, of life and death; judges over all their subjects and in all causes, and yet accountable to none but God only.

Yet James was a capricious ruler, less enlightened than many of the subjects he unjustly ruled. In the new land, therefore, the pioneers luxuriated in their freedom from kings. Their democratic ideals of equality and liberty could flourish where there was no hereditary aristocracy, no divinely-ordained king to rule and overrule. Moreover, they determined that no one could act as king, by that name or any other. Gradually the mechanics of their new democracy were hammered out, so that by the time the Constitution was written, clear-eyed men who understood both the practical necessities of government and the human propensity to abuse power prepared a document to protect men from men.

Man's inherent love of power had to be checked. Jefferson may later claim that "all authority belongs to the people," but that authority would have to be checked somehow. Lord Bryce's famous remark about our Constitution still stands: "It is the work of men who believed in original sin, and were resolved to leave open for transgressors no door which they could possibly shut."

The system worked, and the vote was granted to more and more American citizens through subsequent decades. But in later years the hesitant belief in the ability of people to rule themselves has gradually lost its hesitancy. As early as the latter part of the nineteenth century Matthew Arnold, the English author, warned:

> Whatever one may think of the general danger to the world from the Anglo-Saxon contagion, it appears to me difficult to deny that the growing greatness and influence of the United States does bring with it some danger to the ideal of a high and rare excellence. The average man is too much a religion there; his performance is unduly magnified, his shortcomings are not duly seen and admitted.

By Arnold's day, the average man had become an end in himself; his voice had replaced the voice of God, his sins explained away as just "human nature."

That is a far cry from the cautious hope of the founders that sinful men and women would be able to stifle their selfish impulses sufficiently to live together in harmony. Democracy's problem today is that the hesitancy is gone. Legislators and judges alike have come to believe, or at least act as if they believe, that the voice of the people is the voice of God. Rather than looking to Heaven for guidance or the Scriptures for the basis of law, they look to human precedent and contemporary opinion for judgment. It is the function of government, they believe, to reflect contemporary standards. There is no absolute standard of right and wrong, no supernatural voice, no higher authority to govern human arrogance. Instead, there is general disregard of the religious foundation that brought the country into being. Further, we have forgotten Woodrow Wilson's pertinent warning, "No government has ever been beneficent when the attitude of government was taking care of the people. The only freedom consists in people taking care of the government." So with each passing decade, Big Brother invades increasingly private areas of life, legislating, investigating, deciding.

Watergate was inevitable. When 26 former Nixon aides and agents pleaded guilty or were convicted in the Watergate scandals, Walter Lippmann's comment during the summer of the Ervin committee hearings seemed all the more true: "Watergate shows how very vulnerable our constitutional system is. If the national government falls into the hands of sufficiently unprincipled and unscrupulous men, they can do terrible things before anyone can stop them." Yet most of the convicted men protested their innocence. H. R. (Bob) Haldeman spoke for more than himself when he said, "There's only one human being in the whole world who knows if I'm innocent or guilty. That person is me, and I know that legally and morally I'm totally and absolutely innocent." Perhaps he was. If there is no higher authority than ordinary human behavior, how can we judge him?

That is an interesting question, isn't it? Is there any true standard by which the Watergate defendants, and indeed all government actors and actions, can be judged? What is the role, for example, of the Scriptures, which served as the basis of law for the Pilgrims and Puritans? In the first edition of his English translation of the Scriptures, Wycliffe said, "This Bible is translated and shall make possible Government of people, by people, for people." Although they may not have known that Wycliffe said this, and certainly could not know that Abraham Lincoln would later repeat it, they believed every word of it. America's unprecedented experiment in democracy depended upon Scriptural truth. The early pioneers believed they were establishing a society in America that was strictly in accord with Scripture. As far as they were concerned, their whole concept of democracy came out of the Bible.

Today, however, it plays a minor role in government. It has been replaced by a document which was not designed to have such exalted power, the Constitution of the United States.

Although they would recognize scarcely a phrase in it, most Americans consider the Constitution practically infallible. Every demagogue on any issue knows he can stir the masses by his attack upon the issue's constitutionality. Even Franklin Roosevelt at the height of his personal popularity had to abandon his plan for reorganizing the Supreme Court, because he faced widespread opposition by a nation that believed his plan to be unconstitutional. The fact that his proposed changes did not impinge upon the status of the Court as defined in the Constitution had nothing to do with it; they believed his proposals to be unconstitutional and that was all that mattered.

This is not a twentieth-century reverence. An irony of our history is the fact that in 1861, when the Union was severed by the withdrawal of a group of states, the seceding states wrote their own confederate constitution—and it was almost identical to the federal constitution they were defying.

Subsequent generations have granted the Constitution a reverence that its originators did not have. Governor Morris of Pennsylvania, one of the drafters, spoke for the majority when he said, "While some have boasted it as a work from Heaven, others have given it a less righteous origin. I have many reasons to believe that it is the work of plain honest men, and such, I think, it will appear." Wise old Benjamin Franklin, in appealing for unity in the adoption of the Constitution by the convention, confessed "that there are several parts of this constitution which I do not at present approve, but I am not sure I shall never approve them." He admitted that his advanced age caused him to be a little less sure of his own judgment than when he was younger. So, he said,

> I agree to this Constitution with all its faults, if they are such; because I think a general Government necessary for us, and there is no form of Government but what may be a blessing to the people if well administered for a course of years, and can only end in Despotism, as other forms have done before it, when the people shall have become so corrupted as to need despotic Government, being incapable of any other.

Franklin's claims for the Constitution were only moderate; he knew that the government did not rest on the infallibility of this document, but on the morality of the people. He did not expect a perfect "production" from an assembly of men with "all their prejudices, their passions, their errors of opinion, their local interests, and their selfish views."

Thanks to the good offices of Franklin and others, the Constitution that was written by a disparate group of Americans in 1787 was ratified by a two-thirds majority of the states within a year and became the law of the land. But it has not remained a permanently unchanged law. In a sense it has been remade by every generation of Americans since 1787. The most obvious changes are the Amendments, including the Bill of Rights, which added ten changes almost immediately. But more subtle changes have crept in. Subsequent generations of justices have reinterpreted it according to the prevailing mood of the country at the time. Charles Evans Hughes' famous comment is the truth:

"We are under a Constitution, but the Constitution is what the judges say it is." It has been so from the beginning. In 1803 the first Chief Justice of the Supreme Court, John Marshall, staked out a powerful role for the judiciary branch of government. "It is, emphatically, the province and duty of the judicial department to say what the law is."

No wonder, then, that presidents as early as Thomas Jefferson in 1819 have complained about the courts' heavy hand. When either the legislative or executive branches of government usurp authority, their actions are obvious and immediately correctible. The judiciary, however, operates in the ethereal yet potent atmosphere of ideas and values; its power over the laws and institutions of the nation is insidious. With one decision, as in the 1973 law legalizing abortion, the entire standard of values of the nation can be challenged and the Constitution made to speak to issues which were not at all in the minds of the originators.

The Constitution should serve its original purposes and no more. It is a set of laws and regulations governing the United States; it has to depend on the moral principles of the governed. When the governed turn instead to the Constitution for their moral principles, a vicious cycle is established that can only eventually pull the people down upon themselves. Of the judiciary it is imperative to ask, Who judges the judges? Who restrains the restrainers? When Americans no longer nervously watch for signs of God's disfavor, when He is no longer ultimate judge, then the Supreme Court justices are indeed supreme. There can be no higher appeal. They do in fact determine what law is—and what morality should be. They are the incarnate voice of the people. There is no voice of God.

The inability of a constitution alone to guarantee basic freedoms has been graphically illustrated for us by the Russian form of people's democracy. In the mid-40's *Isvestiya* boasted, "Our greatest happiness is being able to live under the sun of the Stalin constitution, each article of which is sacred for us." We do not need to describe the freedoms the Russian people suffered under Stalin. In 1977 the Brezhnev constitution, with 173 articles, was presented to be rubber-stamped by the supreme Soviet. Its promises are glowing: freedom of press, assembly, religion, and speech, the right to have a house, income, and savings, livestock and "articles of everyday use, and personal consumption and convenience." These and other promises. Then one proviso: "Exercise by citizens of rights and freedoms must not injure the interests of society and the state, and the rights of other citizens." Who decides? The government, of course.

The point of all of this is simply to raise a warning. Any constitution rests upon the principles in which the people really believe. As Mark Van Doren has written, "The Declaration had been ringing first principles about liberty and the rights of man. The Constitution was second thoughts about how that liberty and those rights, once obtained, might be perpetuated in an orderly government." Our Constitution has fulfilled its function admirably. What it cannot do is what it was never intended to do: be a substitute for the Scriptures upon which the Constitution was consciously and subconsciously founded. In spite of their many disagreements at the Convention, the delegates were in basic accord in their belief that Divinity was guiding their destiny and calling them to account, that all men were *created* by that Divinity, that men were made of the breath of Divinity and the dust of the earth, and that although there must be no establishing of a state religion, dependence upon God must never be lost. The Constitution was not intended to supplant Scripture, nor human self-sufficiency to replace humble obedience to God.

From Mission to Maintenance

Believing themselves to be saints in the manner of the earliest Christians, the Mayflower Pilgrims could not submit to the religious authority of their English king. They demanded liberty of conscience and the right to worship in a manner that they believed would please God. For awhile they enjoyed freedom in Leyland, Holland, but farmers could not long be confined in a city—nor could they earn an adequate living. So when an escape to America seemed possible, about forty of these saints crossed to Southampton and boarded the *Mayflower*. Like the children of Israel millennia before them, they left everything they had known in order to become a new people of God.

They did not travel alone. Crowded into the miserably uncomfortable little ship were twice as many Strangers, as the Saints called them, men and women seeking their fortune and, in the opinion of the Saints, unfortunately careless about the faith. The rigid Pilgrims were not prepared to accept the Strangers as Christian equals. Freedom of religion meant the freedom to worship as the Separatists worshiped, or not worship at all. The years would soften their attitude, but, in the meanwhile, they were responding in kind to what they had received at the hands of the established church and its monarch.

Tension mounted as the Mayflower made its fitful way across the turbulent sea. As she dropped anchor, mutiny was brewing among the Strangers. Something had to be done, and it was. A simple document was drafted which everyone aboard signed. Saints and Strangers alike became constituted into a "civil body politic" to be governed by just and equal laws.

In this remarkable document can be seen the presuppositions upon which the new nation would be founded. It was acclaimed almost two centuries later by John Quincy Adams to be "the finest example in modern times of a social compact or system of government instituted by voluntary agreement, conformably to the laws of nature, by men of equal rights and about to establish community in a new country." Here is the compact:

> *In the name of God, Amen.* We whose names are underwritten, *the loyal subjects of our dread sovereign Lord, King James,* by the grace of God, of Great Britain, France, and Ireland king, defender of the faith, etc., having undertaken, for the *glories of God,* and *advancement of the Christian faith,* and *honor of our king and country,* a voyage to *plant the first colony in the northern* parts of Virginia, do by these presents *solemnly and mutually in the presence of God, and of one another, covenant and combine* ourselves together into a civil body politic, for our *better ordering and preservation and furtherance of the ends aforesaid;* and by virtue hereof to enact, constitute, and frame such just and equal laws, ordinances, acts, constitutions, and offices, from time to time, as shall be thought most meet and convenient for the general good of the Colony, unto which we promise all due submission and obedience. In witness whereof we have hereunder subscribed our names at Cape Cod the 11 of November, in the year of the reign of our sovereign Lord, King James of England, France, and Ireland the eighteenth, and of Scotland the fifty-fourth. Anno Dom. 1620.

The underscoring is mine, to call attention to the underlying principles of these pilgrims, which would later be heard in the halls of Philadelphia at the writing of the Declaration of Independence and the Constitution of the United States. They would be uttered again by the towering Civil War president, but they can only scarcely be discerned in the vastly altered atmosphere of the late twentieth century.

In the name of God, Amen

"In the beginning God . . ." "In the beginning was the Word . . ." They were, after all, saints, God's especially chosen people. There could be no question that God governs in the affairs of men and nations—*these* men and the nation *they* were establishing.

loyal subjects of our dread sovereign

Although Separatists and "heretics" they were, they could not dispute Romans 13. They believed that the higher authorities were established by God; they were not revolutionists—yet. Their descendants could only become so when they were convinced that their king was acting contrary to God's will.

for the glories of God, and advancement of the Christian faith and honor of our king and country.

Unlike their greedier compatriots who attempted to settle Jamestown, they did not travel primarily to seek their fortune. They wanted to be faithful to God's will. They sought to extend the kingdom of God, and they hoped to bring honor (in the eyes of God as well as the King) to their country.

to plant the first colony in the northern parts of Virginia.

They knew they were pathfinders. No precedent could guide them. They had no charter to settle at Plymouth (their commission was to establish a colony in Virginia); they had no established political hierarchy to govern them. They were pioneers in land and law.

solemnly and mutually in the presence of God, and of one another, (do) covenant and combine ourselves.

As a body of equals, they entered into a twofold agreement: they would serve God, and they would serve one another. To do so they would "enact, constitute, and frame such just and equal laws, ordinances, acts, constitutions, and offices" that would serve the good of the colony. Individual rights would be subordinate to the good of the colony. Obedience could be expected.

Again unlike the Jamestown experiment, within three years, through their ceaseless effort and their equally untiring prayers, they had indeed established a colony. These hardworking, fun-loving, brightly-attired Pilgrims and their fellow settlers were fulfilling their covenant: They served God and each other. Further, they established precedents that would serve the colonies and the succeeding nation for generations.

Although the Mayflower Compact seems an amazing little document today, it was not an idea peculiar to the Pilgrims. They had been nurtured on Scriptures in which no idea is more fundamental than that of covenant. The Old and New *Testaments* are really the Old and New *Covenants*. The Bible teaches that God established a covenant with Adam in the garden, with Abraham as progenitor of a great people, with Moses at Sinai, and with David as king over Israel. Christ established a New Covenant between God and man on the cross. Each of these covenants had both vertical (that is, between God and man) and horizontal (man with man) dimensions.

The God of the covenants—and of the special covenant with this Pilgrim band—was as He had always been, a hidden and inexpressible essence. But He had revealed himself through His Word, and in His covenant relationships He had freely taken upon himself a name and a people. Since they saw themselves as a new nation of Israel, the Pilgrims adopted the seventeenth chapter of Genesis as their key text, for as Abraham walked by faith to found a new nation, so they had done.

The early colonists believed that their work in America was for God, and what they did for Him and the English nation from which they were not yet severed was vitally important. This sense of their importance derived from their Puritan doctrine, which taught that each person was a significant if sinful contributor to the fulfillment of God's purposes on earth. He had to do his duty to God and his fellowman.

Reformed theology, particularly that of John Calvin (1509-64), stressed this binding and governing covenant of a Christian with his God and his brethren. Historian Leopold von Ranke, in assessing Calvin's contribution to the new world, scarcely exaggerates when he says, "John Calvin was the virtual founder of America." As thoroughgoing Calvinists, our fathers believed they had a special agreement with God; they were acting out their destiny as His people.

Having drawn up their Mayflower Compact, they then established the first democratic community in the New World. They also structured their Congregational Churches on a democratic basis because leaders like John Cotton and Thomas Hooker insisted that the organizations they perceived in the New Testament churches be imitated in the colonies. In this and in other matters, they were radicals, determined to get to the root of everything.

They were radically conservative, however, aiming not to destroy
but to restore the early church and form a society in which one
could lead the New Testament life.

They had no use for sluggards in this effort. Calvin had taught
them that one could serve God as well in business or profession as
through the church. All callings were equally honorable in God's
sight, but sloth was not. The covenant demanded that each individual do his share and be cognizant of the needs of his fellows.
Further, it taught that a man had a right to practice his trade
without having to ask permission of a feudal lord or king—or a
labor union or licensing bureau. It did not forbid the free pursuit
of work on the one hand or offer dole to those who would not
work on the other. The modern welfare society would baffle these
hardy covenanters.

This brand of energetic Puritanism, with its union of faith and
works, was precisely what was needed to tame the rugged terrain
of New England. Stewardship of time as well as money was
preached. "Never waste precious time" became an American
byword that has long survived its Puritan origins. Thanks to the
emphasis upon the horizontal relationships in the covenant, a
spirit of teamwork developed alongside rugged individualism.
They were laying the foundation of democracy.

But they never forgot God. Upon their arrival the Mayflower
passengers thanked God—and continued to do so throughout
their early struggles. Years later at the inauguration of the first
administration of the United States, George Washington gave
voice to a nation's gratitude:

> No people can be bound to acknowledge and adore the Invisible Hand
> which conducts the affairs of man more than those of the United States.
> Every step by which we have advanced to the character of an indepen-
> dent nation seems to have been distinguished by some token of provi-
> dential agency.

Washington could have given full credit to his hardworking and
hard-fighting compatriots during the revolutionary struggle, but
like his forebearers he had an overpowering sense that God had
taken special interest in America. The "chosen people" theme
had not been lost.

By the middle of the nineteenth century, however, our other
great president, still sharing the earliest settlers' basic faith in

God's providence, realistically modified America's claim on God. As president-elect he spoke in Trenton on February 21, 1861:

> I am exceedingly anxious that this Union, the Constitution, and the liberties of the people shall be perpetuated in accordance with the original idea for which that struggle was made, and I shall be most happy indeed if I shall be an humble instrument in the hands of the Almighty, and of this, his *almost chosen people*, for perpetuating the object of that great struggle.

With characteristic humility, Lincoln did not equate America with Israel or presume to say specifically what God had never said, so he inserted his precise "almost." Yet he believed in America's mission and wanted to perpetuate it. After several years of internecine struggle, and with victory for the union assured, he more confidently applied the analogy with ancient Israel:

> I shall need, too, the favor of that Being in whose hands we are, who led our fathers, *as Israel of old*, from their native land and planted them in a country flowing with all the necessaries and comforts of life.

As far as Lincoln was concerned, America was not just another nation among nations, but in a special way especially protected by God for reasons of His own.

In the nation's great moments—the early settlements, the struggle for independence and establishing of the government, the war between the states and subsequent reconciliation—the outstanding leaders have confessed a dependence upon God and a belief that this land has a special God-given mission. When that mission has been forgotten, and when God has been ignored, we have indeed been a nation like any other, as corrupt, as cynical, as selfish as the rest. As man's sense of responsibility to God and society grows dimmer, then politics becomes a game in which winning counts for everything, might makes right, political power is used to conceal rather than expose crime and to perpetuate injustice rather than eradicate it. As deTocqueville warned, "When America ceases to be good, it will cease to be great." Theodore Roosevelt later added, "The things that will destroy America are prosperity-at-any-price, safety-first instead of duty-first, the love of soft living and the get-rich-quick theory of life."

Then Watergate becomes merely a "deplorable incident," or "worse than a crime . . . a blunder," as Richard Nixon confessed.

A country without a mission becomes a country with a burning need to maintain the status quo. Sacrifice for a cause is replaced with machinery to satisfy creature comforts. That is why Watergate was a genuine crisis for America, even though our less-zealous allies were puzzled by our outrage. Sensitive Americans realized that our constitutional, political, and moral values were at stake. We began to recognize again that democratic government rests on the reliable morality of the people; there is no other guarantee. And morality rests on God and mission.

Dietrich Bonhoeffer, observing America as an objective outsider in the 1930's and 1940's, in his *Ethics* contrasts America's democracy and that attempted by the French shortly after the War of Independence. Whereas American democracy was founded upon the kingdom of God and the limitation of all earthly power by the sovereignty of God, France tried to found a democracy upon emancipated man. The nightmare of post-revolutionary France is proof of the insufficiency of the foundation. In America and other Anglo-Saxon countries, however, when democracy is regarded as the Christian form of the state, it rests on the idea that "the Kingdom of God cannot be built by the authority of the state but only by the congregation of the faithful." It is the task of the church, Bonhoeffer believes, to proclaim the principles of social and political order, and of the state to provide the technical means of putting the principles into effect. He claims that it is "enthusiastic spiritualism" that is the determining factor in American thought.

If Bonhoeffer is right, then American democracy can survive only to the extent that spiritual values prevail. God remains faithful to His covenanted promises; so must we. We shall look as always to our government to lead the nation since, as Justice Brandeis has written, "Our government is the potent, the omnipresent teacher." But in its pedagogical role, the government in all its branches, especially in the judiciary, must never fail to recall the nation to its God-given mission. In the name of God, we seek to establish liberty and justice for all.

This chapter is too brief to elaborate the means for restoring our threefold loss. It is hoped that the American people, guided by enlightened leaders, will pledge themselves to a new agreement with God and one another; that we will repent of our arrogance and adopt a more seemly posture of humility before God and His revealed Word; that we will provide in wisdom and temperance for the well-being of our posterity; and that we will again grasp

the truth that whenever God has called a people He has charged
that people not only to be blessed but to bless, not to be served but
to serve. Those who brought our nation to birth based their actions on moral and spiritual principles. They were a Pilgrim people on a mission for God. Somewhere along the way that early
vision became cloudy, and the pioneer's descendants began to
daydream in the hypnotic enchantment of prosperity. Raucous
noises have now rudely awakened us from our reverie. Encroach-
ing dangers surround us. Only vision can save us now, a vision
like the one that led our ancestors across an ocean and into a
covenant, a vision, to become a people of God.

Freedom and License

by Knofel Staton

Freedom.

Nations go to war in order to get it or keep it. Children run away from home in search for their idea of it. Married couples divorce to participate in their definition of it. Indebted people declare bankruptcy to feel their idea of it. Some people move to the city for anonymity—another idea of freedom. Others move to the country to fewer pressures and more flexible schedules—another concept of freedom. Others live morally reckless lives, experimenting with the unrestrained expressions of inner passions—to find their idea of freedom.

America and Freedom

"Americans" have always been concerned about freedom; they were concerned about it even before they became a country. The Declaration of Independence announced the dissolvement of political bonds with England and the establishment of a separate and equal nation that would be founded on certain self-evident truths: "that all men are created equal; that they are endowed by their Creator with certain inalienable rights; that among these, are life, liberty, and the pursuit of happiness."

The emphasis upon liberty was the initial concern in the writing and designing of the Constitution of the United States of America, which begins with these words:

We the people of the United States, in order to form a more perfect union, establish Justice, insure domestic Tranquility, provide for the common defense, promote the general Welfare, and secure the Blessings of Liberty to ourselves and our Posterity, do ordain and establish this Constitution of the United States of America.

From the outset of our country's independence, we connected our search for liberty with two different poles—our Creator (outside and above us) and our own pursuit for happiness (within ourselves). The question is: Can these two extremes actually be lived out together in harmony?

The answer depends on how we define liberty and happiness. Some people make the two words synonymous. They say, "We are totally happy when we are totally free." Yet the Preamble to the Constitution admits that liberty is to bring justice, tranquility, and welfare to *all*. How can such blessings come to *all* if each person is unrestrained and allowed to do as he wishes? Won't someone get hurt or stepped on while others are doing what they want?

Ironically, the nation that seems to be the most concerned about freedom seems to understand it least of all (or as inadequately as other nations). Our nation has failed to realize that the only way our freedoms can be perpetuated and protected is by the acknowledgement of absolutes—the absolutes communicated to us by our Creator. When society is stripped of these absolutes, then freedom is only for the person or country that has the most power. When the "curbs" that keep freedom in check are gone, then man himself becomes the authority and decides who is right and wrong. Each person becomes "right" in his own eyes.

When such individualism pervades a nation's thinking, we are left with two alternatives: The first is to allow the law of the survival of the fittest to reign. This philosophy does not accept man as one who is created by God or in God's image. Man is thought of as a machine or an animal; he is stripped of value. Thus society can do whatever it wants with man—manipulate him, own him, decide whether he lives or dies, interchange his parts, and even take vital parts from a "worn-out" man to help another "machine" (man) who is of more value. Society can even put the antiques (older persons) on a junk pile with others of their kind because they are no longer useful to society. Children do not have to provide for their elderly parents—why be so inconvenienced? Parents no longer have to provide such watchful care over their children; they can let an agency of society do it—why be so inconvenienced? Or if society thinks an infant might be born with a malfunction, the life of the fetus can be terminated through abortion (after all, the fetus is a non-person, society thinks)—why be inconvenienced by people who are "not quite right"?

The longer such actions are taken without being condemned, the more seared our consciences will become. Eventually the "liberty" given to us by the government will be decided by us citizens as the right thing to do (that is, abortion becomes right because it is legal). When society accepts this kind of treatment of people, our freedoms have become license to do whatever we wish to each other—and it will be legal. Hitler believed and applied this philosophy (survival of the fittest), which led to the near annihilation of an entire race.

The second alternative is to allow the law of society to reign. This is the philosophy that the consensus of society decides what is right and wrong. When a segment of society wants to pursue their own interests, they seek to make new laws or go to the courts to have laws interpreted in a way that will support their wishes. Consequently, if anyone tries to hinder another person from pursuing his own happiness, the matter goes before the court; then the court decides what is right or wrong. A court that does not accept absolutes will become permissive and will give license to whatever a person wants to do.

For instance, each person in America has the freedom of speech. A certain segment of society wanted to speak dirty, smutty, and crude language. They went to court to determine their rights. The court said censorship is denying freedom; so the smutty language is made legal. Now filthy language has filtered into almost every area of our lives—entertainment, art, music, the mass media, literature, and school textbooks.

My wife and I went to a very good movie recently. It had a good script, a good group of actors, and fine cinematography; but cuss words were interspersed throughout. Those words did not fit the plot or the characters. It was quite apparent that the crude language was "stuck in" because it was legal and was expected by the masses. Such excessive use of this language in all areas of the mass media cannot help but affect the way our growing children will talk in the years to come.

What has happened in the turning of the freedom of speech into license (for anyone to say anything he pleases) is also happening in the way we look at sex, marriage, and divorce. Our courts say divorce is all right and does not hurt anyone. Now with the no-fault divorces, there is not even anyone to blame. Divorce has become the acceptable and sensible thing to do—even in Christian circles. Pornography and massage parlors can move into a community, and the courts decide—all in the name of freedom—that a person's sex life is his own private business. The courts decide that homosexuality hurts no one and that each person has the right to live as he wishes. And before long, the major portion of society will accept these sexual perversions (adultery, pornography, and homosexuality) as "alternative lifestyles." Even Christians are saying, "do whatever makes you happy." What is non-acceptable Biblically has become acceptable and permitted in society because the majority of people say it is all right. We are allowing society to tell us by a popular vote what is right and wrong and what will or will not hurt anyone.

A recent decision by the Supreme Court protects a teenager's "freedom" by ruling that she does not have to get parental consent for an abortion. Such decisions open the door to further alienation in parent-child relationships. I asked our circuit judge what such a ruling would mean if children decided to go to court to keep parents from hindering their "freedom" to come home any hour they wished, or to not go to church if they did not want to, or to refrain from or engage in certain activities. He replied, "With the same reasons cited for bypassing the parents in the question of abortion, the children would legally win the case." There are no limits to what children could do—all in the name of freedom.

The problem with this philosophy of the law of society is that often the majority of people are wrong. Hitler was supported by the majority of the German people; large groups of people support Reverend Moon; many people supported the work of Jim Jones. In the Bible, God commanded the people to conquer the promised land. But the people formed a committee to make a feasibility study. The majority voted *not* to enter the promised land, but the majority was wrong. On another occasion, King Ahab got four hundred prophets to approve his decision; only one prophet had other ideas. The vote was four hundred to one, but the four hundred were wrong—the lone prophet was right.

As long as absolutes that are based on God's Word are not accepted as the authority for society, our nation will continue to decline morally. And as long as we rationalize away Biblical standards and say we are giving all people "liberty," we will be weakening the church. When we let society tell us what is right and wrong or decide that men are merely machines, then our liberties will indeed be turned into license. And through it all, our consciences will be clear; we will tell ourselves, "no one is getting hurt, and after all, it is legal."

If we cannot trust our government, the courts, or our society to properly guard and curb our liberty, where can we turn? Where can we find the true freedom that will lead to the welfare and pursuit of happiness for each and every person?

True Freedom

God is the absolute authority who will protect us in our liberty. He has shown us the way for true freedom in His Word. He has outlined clearly the meaning and applications of true liberty. He has communicated the proper and workable "curbs" that will insure the right use of liberty that will benefit and protect all mankind.

In creation. Man was originally created in the image and likeness of God; he has the ability to think, to reason, to make decisions. He was created to be and act like God. God took a risk when He made man with a mind and a will, for man had the freedom to choose not to obey God, to turn away from God's will. Adam and Eve had freedom in the Garden of Eden; there was only one law to abide by. But that law was tied to liberty, for they had the freedom to break it.

The devil sought to get them to turn their liberty into license. He told them they would be better off if they did "their own thing" instead of God's will. He successfully convinced Adam and Eve to use their freedom to please themselves (Genesis 3:4, 5), and in that act they sinned.

Sin damaged their inner natures, just as it has to all mankind ever since. In the sinful state, man is not free to function as God had designed him to function. He is malfunctioning and enslaved to a life of selfishness. A malfunctioning carburetor is not free to function according to the specifications and expectations of the manufacturer. In a similar way, sin changes our inner natures so that we cannot function properly.

Even though man made the choice to do things his own way, God still loved him and did not want him to be fettered in the shackles of sin forever. He promised to send His own Son to free man once again to function as he should. He wanted to enable man's original designed nature to be restored, so He would send the Liberator, Jesus Christ.

The law. Man's original nature was to relate to God and to others with love, God's kind of love—a love that is unselfish and other-oriented. It was a love that causes one to act responsibly. It was not the love that causes us to think only of what return we will get for ourselves or merely the affectionate love between friends. God's kind of love sees a need and moves to meet that need without considering what the cost might be or whether the other person is worthy or not. It is a love that causes one to make decisions with the other person's well-being in mind.

But man's freedom to love in such a way was perverted by sin. Thus for a time, God had to teach man what this type of love is and how it was to be applied in his daily life, so he would be ready to receive the freedom that the Liberator would bring and be able to handle that freedom with responsibility. God instructed man about love and responsibility through the Law of the Old Testament.

Every minute detail of the law had to do with love and showed how much God cared about what happened to man. The people had to be taught how to treat each other and how to relate to God properly. They were even instructed about returning a lost ox to its owner. Without this teaching, they would have had their own private oxen barbeques at the expense of their neighbors. The law served to keep men in check. God used the law to restrain men from changing their freedom into license and destroying themselves and all of mankind before Christ came. The law served as man's protection from his own selfish desires in the interim period before Christ. The law was the boundary or guardrail that would keep men on the right road that would eventually lead to Christ, who would show them the ultimate expression of God's kind of love.

Christ, liberty, and love. Christ came to set us free from the slavery of sin and the resulting malfunctioning of our natures. When Christ came, the interim period was over; true freedom was here. He released man from the burdens of the law and freed man to think and act in accordance with his created nature.

But He did not just free us *from* something; He also freed us *to* something. He freed us to live out the true meaning of love in God's way. He put a new life inside of us; this new life would restore our original natures so that we could once again be able to think and act with God's characteristics. That new life within us is the Spirit of God himself. The Spirit restores God's original character in us, and the first dimension of that character is love (Galatians 5:22-25). The Spirit equips us to live for others, and in that type of living, we find freedom from our selfishness—which is true freedom. "And where the Spirit of the Lord is, there is liberty" (2 Corinthians 3:17).

The paradox. Christ brings true freedom, but it is not synonymous with license, with total independence, or with autonomy (self-rule). Christ releases us from sin and from the restraints of the Old Testament law, yes; but He is not setting us free to "do our own thing."

In their desire to have freedom, humans have listened to many counterfeit claims as the way to freedom. These opponent mavericks have enticed us, "promising them freedom while they themselves are slaves of corruption; for by what a man is overcome, by this he is enslaved" (2 Peter 2:19, *New American Standard Bible*). Those who think total autonomy is the way to freedom have become humanity's most fettered and restricted people. They have become imprisoned into the littleness of the "cell" of self. In the name of freedom they have become fettered to a grand style of living or to always having to live to impress others. Some have gotten chained to perverted sexual habits. Some have fallen prey to the drug culture and to the thrill of the sensational.

A life of seemingly total independence is really a life of slavery—slavery to self. Life becomes restricted by the passions of self, and man caught in its clutches can become no better or larger than his own self interests. That type of restricted existence is a foretaste of death; we could call it "a living death."

False freedom locks a person into himself, while true freedom through Christ broadens a person to live with and for others. Christ has set us free to live His way, to live doing "His thing." Doing things Jesus' way is freedom? It sounds contradictory, doesn't it? But it is really God's consideration and love for us that causes Him to want us to go His way instead of ours. He knows what will lead to our well-being and happiness, and He knows that self-rule is not the way.

Thus, this true freedom we have through Christ is not boundless. It has clearly defined restraints: live in such a way that you serve God and others out of your pure love for them. This type of liberty frees us from serving self so that we can serve others. We will not use our liberty to satisfy our selfish interests: "For you were called to freedom, brethren, only do not turn your freedom into an opportunity for the flesh, but through love serve one another" (Galatians 5:13, *NASB*). Imagine that! Using the terms "freedom" and "servant" in the same sentence!

Our new life of service springs from our love; it comes out of the spontaneous desire of love, not out of a burdensome duty of law. With the Holy Spirit within us, we are no longer restrained from killing, lying, and gossiping because we have memorized a law; but because we love others and we know how hurtful these actions are to others. This type of restraint is always more effective than that which is forced upon us by the law.

I cannot remember my mother ever "laying down the law" that I had to be home at a certain time, or that I must never take a drink of alcohol, or that I must never go into that "den of iniquity" on Main Street—the pool hall. Why didn't she? Wasn't she concerned about me? Or was she a loose woman herself? No, my mother was a righteous woman, and there was never a doubt that she loved me. She only had an eighth-grade education, but she knew that love was the best guard over my behavior.

Although she never set a deadline for how late I could stay out, I always came home at a time when I thought she would want me to. I only tasted from a bottle of wine once in high school, and I never stepped into that pool hall. Why? Not because of some law that she handed down, but because I loved my mother and did not want to do anything that would hurt her. I knew that she would not sleep if I stayed out until the early hours of the morning. I knew that if I drank or went into the pool hall I would be driving a "knife" into my mother's heart. I could have turned my liberty into license, but my love for my mother kept me from doing so.

I saw the concept of love over law work in the military service also. I was a sergeant and stationed in Japan. In addition to my regular duties, I was put in charge of a barracks. I did not want that assignment, for that particular barracks had the reputation of being the worst on the base. Every morning for a couple of years, the preceding barracks' chief had to take at least one person to the colonel for disciplinary action. Chairs would go through windows. Drinking and gambling went on until the wee hours. One fellow from that barracks was under "house arrest." He was the first military person scheduled to be tried for murder in a Japanese civil court. Not only that, but an entire wing of the barracks had segregated themselves from all the others. That group was filled with big, black rebels. I was only 5 feet 7 inches tall and weighed 145 pounds; I'm telling you—I was scared! I simply valued my life too much to want to move to that barracks, but I didn't know how to say "no" to a colonel.

However, the next year turned out to be a delight instead of a nightmare. I decided to treat the fellows in that barracks differently than they had been treated before. I told them that the barracks was to be their "home away from home," and I had the building painted and repaired. I made it clear that I wanted to know them and that I wanted to be their friend. I told them to call me "Buddy" after the duty hours were over (with a name like Knofel I had to have a nickname). I kept my door open and invited the fellows to come in and talk. I learned all their first names. The tension began to ease.

When it was time for the commander to inspect the barracks, the men did not do any better job than usual to get the building ready. My assistant and I never said a word, but we remade every bed that needed it. We put all the unshined shoes and the stray socks into a locker in my room and padlocked it. We passed the inspection, and afterwards we put up a list of all those whose beds had to be remade. We told all those who had some missing gear that it was in the sergeant's room for them to claim. There were no harsh words spoken, no condemnations given out. Within three weeks, the men in the barracks were passing the inspections themselves without any help from us.

A hard-nosed policy was changed to a concerned-heart policy. Those fellows could have "punched out" such a softie, but they didn't. When they were no longer faced with a power image, they no longer felt the need to rebel. Not one man in that year had to be taken to the Colonel for discipline. Some abused the liberty I allowed them, but most of them acted responsibly; they became governed by respect and love, not by laws.

Living for others out of love will cause us to go beyond what any law would require. This truth was recently demonstrated at our college. No one had ever punched a time clock at our college; those who worked by the hour always kept track of the hours they worked and then signed a time sheet. Recently it was decided it would probably be more businesslike to have the cafeteria workers punch a time clock. But at the end of the semester, the cafeteria was five thousand dollars in the red for the first time in many years. Why? Inflation in food costs? No, it was the use of the time clock.

Prior to having the time clock, many of the workers worked through their lunch hours and overtime voluntarily and did not ask to be paid for that time. They were sacrificing for the benefit of the college. But with the use of the time clock, every minute spent on the job was accounted for and had to be paid for. The opportunity of service for others was taken away when the freedom to come and go was legalized.

The apostle Paul spoke about the paradox of liberty and the law. In 1 Corinthians 9:1, he asked, "Am I not free?" In the following verses, he listed some of the freedoms he had, and then he observed, "But I have used none of these things" (9:15). Why didn't he? Because of the love he felt for the people and for the Lord. "For though I am free from all men, I have made myself a slave to all, that I might win the more" (9:19, *NASB*).

When God unlocked the chain of His law, He put within us the constraint of His own nature—the Holy Spirit. So that we could live responsibly because we *want* to, not because we *have* to. Love motivates us, not the law. Why do we think we need to obey God's commands in the Bible then? Because such restraints guide the demonstration of our love. That is why the New Testament contains guidelines for our new life in Christ. It is one thing to want to love our fellowmen, but it is quite another to know what the content of that love is—to know what I must do or not do to enhance another's well-being. The person with the true freedom found in Christ will want to have guidelines. He will not want to be left floundering around or hurting others without realizing it or without intending to do so. God did not give us these commands to squash us or hold us down; neither does He want us to be burdened by an excessive system of legalism; but He does want us to know when our freedom hurts someone else. That is why the Christians' declaration of independence from the law (in Romans and Galatians) is followed closely by practical guidelines about how to live out that freedom.

To summarize, notice the differences between counterfeit freedom and true freedom:

Counterfeit Freedom	*True Freedom*
Live for self	Live for others
Total license	Total love
Do your own thing	Do God's will
Let passions control you	Let Christ control you
Unrestrained	Within boundaries
Autonomous	Theonomous

Freedom, Flexibility, and Fetters

There are guidelines included in Christian liberty, but there is also much flexibility. Where there are no specific commands to live in certain ways or no specific prohibitions, we have the freedom to be flexible. God has decided for us what is moral and what is immoral and stated these clearly in His Word. Everything else is amoral (neither moral nor immoral in and of themselves). In this amoral category, we have flexibility.

This flexibility covers most of our daily expressions. Can a person play pool, dance, drink wine, go to a movie, or miss a worship service? Can the order of a worship service be altered? Can we lift our hands in prayer or should we kneel? Are we to worship on only a certain day of the week, or can we worship at other times? Can we eat all kinds of food? What we do in these areas has not been covered in Scriptural commands, thus we have flexibility.

We can handle this freedom and flexibility in three ways: (1) We can seek always to serve God and others out of love; (2) we can devise man-made laws to insure that God's family members will not overstep God's boundaries; (3) we can turn our liberty into license and seek to get by with as much as we can. God's will is that we do the first alternative. He wants us to learn to live responsibly out of love, not out of man-made commands. Neither does He want us to use our flexibility to be selfish and hurt ourselves and our fellowmen.

The legalists. There will always be those people who want to limit all our freedoms. They are so legalistically minded that they will set up laws for every minute action and then judge others by the laws they themselves have devised. They rush in to clamp on the fetters as soon as Jesus has broken them.

For instance, we are told not to neglect the assembling of ourselves together (Hebrews 10:25). But some men have added on to that guideline, and say that every Christian should be in the church building twice on Sunday and once on Wednesday. Then they judge and evaluate who is truly Christian by how many times they attend all these services. The legalists have made up an ordinance (it need not be written down), and then judge others by how they live it out. God gives us freedom, but the legalists burden us with more rules and make us feel guilty.

We are also told in the Scripture not to lust after a woman in our minds or actions. But legalists have come along and added rules to that guideline. They say it is a sin to dance, a sin to go to the beach, and a sin for a woman to wear shorts.

When we do such adding on to God's guidelines and try to legislate people's actions in areas where God has given us freedom, we are slipping back into the legalistic mentality of the Old Testament. We are draining away the most powerful motivating force for responsible living—God's love.

It is always a risk to allow liberty, but it was a risk God was willing to take. We must also take that risk. Yes, some people will abuse it; but that does not give us the right to make up new laws to govern them. It is time that we allowed one another to grow into Christlikeness, not into legalism.

The best way to keep liberty from turning into license is not by setting up a new rule, but by establishing better relationships with one another. Close, loving, and respectful fellowship is the most powerful force to keep us within the God-given boundaries of love. That is why we are encouraged in the Scriptures to fellowship with one another (Hebrews 10:23-25; Ephesians 4:11-16).

Flexibility, but not license. We have the freedom to be angry, but not to sin against someone in that anger (Ephesians 4:26). We have the freedom to work, but not to act selfishly by hoarding possessions (4:28). We have the freedom to speak, but not to hurt someone else with our speech (4:29). We have the freedom to express ourselves and react, but not with destructiveness (4:31—5:2). We have the freedom to decide what we will do with our lives, but not to live immorally (5:3-20). We have the freedom to marry, but not to act selfishly in that relationship (5:21-33). We have the freedom to discipline our children, but not to treat them destructively (6:4). God has freed us to take positions of leadership, but not in order to "lord it over" others (1 Peter 5:2, 3; 2 Corinthians 13:10).

We have the freedom to enjoy sex (1 Corinthians 7), but we do not have the license to do whatever we wish with it. The New

Testament clearly condemns adultery and homosexuality (1 Corinthians 6:9, 10), for they both pervert God's intended design for sex. Adultery breaks the covenant of commitment between a husband and wife and defiles the marriage bed (Hebrews 13:4). Homosexuality turns sex into yielding to selfish passions only. It disregards God's creative design of the male and female (Genesis 2:18; Romans 1:26, 27; 1 Corinthians 7:4).

We have the freedom to enjoy sex within marriage, but again this does not allow us to do whatever we wish sexually within marriage. Between a husband and wife, there are no "unclean" acts *as long as* those acts are *mutual* expressions of love for each other and within God's moral code (no bestiality or trading of partners, for example). The husband and wife express God's kind of love for each other, not thinking or acting selfishly in their sexual intimacies.

Women are to have freedom. Sinful men have sought to imprison women to positions of inferiority for many hundreds of years, but that is one of the shackles Jesus came to unloose. God never intended women to be so hemmed in. He created the female in His image as well as the male (Genesis 1:27). God has always cared for women, sought to protect them, and encouraged them to serve Him with their many abilities. Christ truly liberated women to function with all their femininity, but they are not to live in unrestrained license. Women are not to seek to act, think, and look like the men.

God created male and female to be equal, but different. Erik Erikson suggests that the inner space of a woman that is designed to house and nourish new life is holistically related to the total woman. Whether or not a woman has children, she brings to society the balance of a life-sustaining, life-protecting and caring disposition. Society is at its best when both the female and male dispositions are allowed to be expressed in concert, not in competition.

Erikson also makes the point that a woman should bring her femininity to whatever situation in life she enters—a family, a career, community work, politics, or church work. If she tries to step out of her femininity, she will be stepping outside of her created nature and will lose her freedom to function as a woman. She will become fettered and will be pulling against herself. It is important that women be liberated, but not so they lose their image of femininity and their uniqueness as women.

Men and women were created to be different, but neither is superior to the other. Men have been very slow to admit this fact. Men were given the freedom to exercise leadership in the home and in the community, but they have used it to keep women down. They have passed down traditions and practices that did not come from God. They have misused their freedom, keeping women fenced in regardless of the gate that God has opened.

One tradition is that women are to submit to men in every instance. God did say that wives were to submit to their own husbands, but God never said that *all* women were to be submitted to *all* men. God also said that husbands were to be submissive to their wives because as Christians we are all to submit to one another (Ephesians 5:21).

Even in the marriage relationship, men have used the directions that God gave about submission to lift themselves up to the positions of generals or dictators, so they can "lord it over" another person. They have used God's direction and design to further their own selfish interests.

Men have conveniently failed to understand what God really intends for marriage to be. Jesus made it clear that the husband and wife are to be yoked together, which means they are to be a *team*. They are not to be two independent people pulling in opposite directions seeking to fulfill their own selfish desires. A team that works well together must have a leader, but not a dictator. A dictator will make up rules and force others to obey him out of fear, while a leader will love and care about the welfare of the others on his team. A dictator will view himself as the "boss" and will expect others to do whatever he wishes in blind obedience, no thinking about it—just do it. But a leader will guide, protect, and seek to meet another's needs. In other words, God intended the husband to be a loving, caring, serving leader to the wife. He never intended for husbands to rule over wives with iron fists or for the purpose of fulfilling their desires for power and manipulation of others.

Women as well as men are important members of the body of Christ, and have God-given gifts (1 Corinthians 12; Romans 12). Let us recognize the mutual abilities we have as well as our God-created differences. Women, don't use your freedom to act like men. Men, don't use your freedom to treat women as if they were second-rate. We need each other to make this world what it should be.

We can conclude, then, that the only license we have in our Christian freedom and flexibility is to be and to act like God, to act responsibly, to serve God and others out of love. Therefore if we know that participation in an amoral activity (an area of flexibility, such as playing pool or dancing) would cause someone else, who thought it was a sin, also to participate in it, then in doing it we would be in error. We would be causing a Christian family member to stumble. The best thing to do in this case would be to refrain from that activity (1 Corinthians 8:9; Romans 14:1-23).

At the same time, we must not push this principle to extremes as some do. They say we must never do anything that anyone else thinks is a sin. If we followed that teaching, we would not be able to do much of anything. I could not drive an air-conditioned car because some people think it is a sin to have luxurious items. I could not go to the theater; I could not ever wear anything but a suit and a tie. On and on we could go.

Some people teach we should never do or say anything that would offend anyone. But Jesus, our example, offended people. He did many things that people thought were sinful: He healed on the Sabbath, ate with unwashed hands, ate with sinners, and did not fast on schedule. Jesus knew His actions would not cause them to stumble, and He was demonstrating the flexiblity that God allows. Let us learn to love others as we should and practice discernment in all areas.

Conclusion

As Americans and as Christians, we have many liberties. Our government has assured us liberty, and our God has promised us liberty in Christ. But we must not allow our liberties to be turned into license as a cover-up for the evils of selfish mankind. We must remain faithful to the absolutes of God's Word, regardless of what society thinks about those absolutes. Even if the President, the courts, or the whole community approves, God is the final authority. If He does not approve of an attitude or practice, it is not right. This is the only way we can avoid total destruction of our nation and of ourselves as individuals.

Christians in Politics

by Senator Jesse Helms

During the last 25 years, we have witnessed the most ferocious assault on Christian faith and morals that has occurred in Western civilization since the French Revolution. This attack was first taken up by many in the intellectual community and is now being carried forward by a growing number in government. Especially in the last several years, the federal government has not even tried to conceal its hostility toward Christian values and beliefs.

When Christ was asked to specify the greatest commandment of the law, He told His followers they were to love God with their whole heart and soul and mind and strength, and to love their neighbors as themselves; for love, He said, was the fulfillment of the law.

I spoke a moment ago of the French Revolution. Every student of history is well familiar with its famous watchwords, Liberty, Equality, and Fraternity. From these two imperatives—from the gospel on the one hand, and from modern revolutionary philosophers on the other—have sprung the two antithetical forces contending for dominance in the United States today. The trouble is, in our contemporary situation, it is hard to find one without some admixture of the other, or, should I say, some pretension of the other.

Very often we hear preached from our pulpits a kind of love that is a perversion of the meaning of the word. Certainly secular culture, especially the "entertainment" industry, has done its uttermost to confound what surely is the highest of virtues with the lowest of vices. We must ever and again return to the Scriptures for a true definition of the meaning of love. For unless we do so, it is too easy to be led astray. It is too easy to identify personal gratification, or statist schemes of welfare and pacifism, with Christian love, and to rely on these as substitutes for charity.

Scriptural teaching throughout the ages has stressed the threefold obligation of faith, hope, and charity by which all Christians are bound. But as what one great spiritual writer called "the religion of the world" has increasingly penetrated the thinking of many churchmen, the old virtues of faith, hope, and charity have been supplanted by man-made political ideals. Thus even many Christians have become seduced by left-wing theories of government and social action.

As a result, Christians, anti-Christians, post-Christians, atheists, agnostics, and skeptics all find themselves using the same political vocabulary, but with vastly different concepts behind the words they use. Has this not had the effect of paralyzing, at least to some extent, the Christian camp? They have conceded too much ground to the modern-day "children of darkness," who, as the Lord himself declared, are wiser in their generation than the children of light. Some Christians have been persuaded that they are being exemplary citizens by keeping their convictions about truth, justice, and the nature of man entirely to themselves.

I am no semanticist, but I deal with politics and the vocabulary of politics every working day. My impression is that the traditional American political ideals and even moral ideals have been turned inside out by concepts that derive from the European Enlightenment and its blood-soaked consummation, the French Revolution. Very often I listen in the Senate to speeches and statements and thundering debates about such things as freedom and rights and equality, and the function of government. At such times I feel, as did the sower of the seed in that field where the tares were crowding out the wheat, that "an enemy hath done this." An *enemy* has changed the meaning of these terms to serve quite different ends.

The concept of freedom, upon which our Constitution was based, derives from the usages of English common law, and these were firmly rooted in Scripture and in centuries of precedent. The notions of "freedom" that prevail in our courts today are alien to those that inspired the founding fathers. Contemporary "freedom" is construed as a kind of autonomy in which the individual is free to do as he pleases, regardless of the consequences of others. Beyond this, the citizens at large are seen to have a corollary obligation to finance his doing whatever he pleases.

Similarly, our forebears did indeed recognize the principle of the freedom of the press, but they did not envision that it would be invoked by individuals who felt the need to express themselves by publishing directions for constructing an H-bomb, and that the courts would concur.

Many hours could be spent analyzing the transformation of the concept of *rights* in the last two decades alone. Rights, it seems, have multiplied like rabbits.

The historical conception of rights as being prior to the state, as benefits accruing to individuals because of their status as human beings and children of God, has given way to an idea of rights as claims against the state. Thus we have just discovered tenants' rights, gay rights, convicts' rights, students' rights, and so on.

As columnist Joseph Sobran has observed,

> At a deeper level, the modern world has severed rights from any framework of piety—the sense of a moral order to which man is subordinate. Earlier (and saner) generations would have said that any right to do X depends on whether it is right to do X. In the discussion of things like abortion and homosexuality, we are now urged to be agnostic about right and dogmatic about rights. . . . It is social contract theory run amok.

It has been my overriding goal to reinstitute this "framework" of which Sobran speaks. For years I have done my best to urge Christians to throw off the constraints that others have imposed upon them—or that they have imposed upon themselves by interpreting our history and our system of government in secularist, liberal, and rationalist terms. It is now time for Christians to redefine the terms of the debate, and to reaffirm the spiritual heritage of the country.

Too often we hear the charge that in a "pluralistic" society, it is not proper for Christians to assert their values and their interests in public policy discussions. But where in the whole history of the foundation of the country do you find any mention of this "pluralism," which overrides every other value?

Did we fight the war for independence, or any other war, in

order to establish "pluralism?" Surely not, because "pluralism" is a creation of modern liberals who wanted to remake society in their own image; but before they could do so, it was necessary to anesthetize certain segments of the population who had unacceptable notions about such realities as God, the family, and property. This was done by promoting the notion of "pluralism." Wheras America had always been an open society where freedom of religion and freedom of conscience were guaranteed to all, "pluralism" subverted this by confining religion, and hence morality, to private matters, thus effectively barring both from any influence on public policy.

Pluralism, then, was the device used by the proponents of secular humanism, the lineal descendants of the French revolutionaries, to derail Christian participation in government, while the social gospel was simultaneously promoted as the means by which Christian energies would be directed in ways acceptable to them. So pluralism paved the way for the virtual *monopoly* status that secular humanism enjoys in the United States today.

From 1933, when the first Humanist Manifesto was published, until 1973, when the Humanist Manifesto II—as militantly atheist a document as was its predecessor—came out, this philosophy flourished. To this day it is still the philosophic foundation of the academic community, the federal bureaucracy, and the judiciary.

The success of secular humanism as a set of assumptions for the majority of people working in these institutions has forced Christian principles outside the mainstream of much of American life. It is a serious question whether the new public orthodoxy of secular humanism will tolerate any public Christian activity contrary to its principles. However, Christians who are willing to compromise their Christianity to act in accordance with the tenets of a revolutionary humanism are often spared criticism and even applauded for their great Christian conscience.

Perhaps one of the best financed allegedly religious organizations with a long history of involvement in political affairs is the World Council of Churches, which receives more than half of its American contributions from the United Methodist Church and the United Presbyterian Church. During 1978 the World Council of Churches gave $85,000 to the guerrilla organizations that composed the Patriotic Front of Zimbabwe (Rhodesia). The donation came after a two-year series of atrocities in which terrorists of the Patriotic Front murdered 33 Christian missionaries and their children, and just before the terrorists shot down two unarmed Air Rhodesia commercial airliners carrying civilians and then massacred the passengers who survived the crash.

Yet few of those American commentators who are now so concerned about the involvement of evangelical churchmen in politics raised their voices to protest or even question this financing of terrorism. Their silence is astounding, since the Communist-organized Patriotic Front was attempting through these acts to depose the government of a pro-American black African bishop in the Methodist Church, Abel Muzorewa.

Around the world the persecution of Christian minorities—whether it be the murder of missionaries in Rhodesia, the program of genocide against Christians in Uganda, the systematic destruction of Christian communities in Lebanon, or the imprisonment of Christians in the Soviet Union—continues on a regular basis without much concern on the part of the United States government or the other secular Western democracies.

Within the United States not only has secular humanism been adopted as the new public philosophy, but the ability and right of Christians to preserve their own spiritual heritage and fulfill their mission of evangelization has been threatened by government actions to regulate Christian schools and restrict evangelists in the use of television and radio. If these developments continue, Christians may soon have to ask whether there will be room for them in American society during the next 25 years.

The involvement of leading evangelical and fundamentalist churchmen in the public debate concerning the right of voluntary school prayer, the independence of church-related schools, and the immorality of abortion is a new sign that the community of Christians in the United States will not permit themselves to be forced into exile in their own country.

Throughout history, times of great adversity have witnessed equally great times of spiritual awakening. I believe that such a spiritual rebirth is occurring in the United States today. The fifty million evangelical and fundamentalist Christians in our country today are "sleeping giants of American politics." Such a spiritual revival inevitably must affect the political process, although the prevailing secular humanists will attempt to contain it. Christians must not hesitate to insist that their right of religious expression and of evangelization be respected. Nor should they hesitate to use the political process to defend those rights.

When I was elected to the Senate in 1972, I made a personal commitment to do my best to restore the right of voluntary prayer to our schoolchildren. I knew it would be rough going—and it has been. However, I sensed that if I persisted in my efforts and required the members of the Senate to take a position, repeatedly, on this question—the people of this country would take note of how their senators were voting.

This is precisely what happened. Each time I forced a vote on the question, a few more senators were persuaded by their constituents to re-evaluate their position. Finally, in 1979, the Senate approved an amendment to restore voluntary prayer.

To me and to many of my colleagues in the Senate, the issue of voluntary prayer in schools is larger than the fundamental constitutional right of the free exercise of religion. It represents a profound conflict between secular humanism and Christianity in the United States.

The founding fathers had no intention of forbidding prayer in the schools. So often the First Amendment is cited by those who oppose school prayer. But they are wrong, as many constitutional scholars now acknowledge. When the Bill of Rights was being drafted, the first proposed wording of the First Amendment read: "Congress shall make no law *touching* religion." But that proposal was defeated, because the founding fathers did not want to shut religion out of our national life. Their only intent was to protect the American people from an established national church—a church that would be controlled and paid for by government. If that original proposal had been adopted, then prayer in the schools would indeed be subject to question.

Instead, the familiar wording of the First Amendment was approved: "Congress shall make no law respecting *an establishment* of religion." In other words, the First Amendment was clearly directed at a government-controlled church and a government-financed church. In fact, the very day that Congress passed the First Amendment, Congress called on President Washington to proclaim a national day of prayer. The authors of the Constitution believed that religion ought to receive encouragement from government in a manner not incompatible with the private rights of conscience.

But, if the Supreme Court's prayer decisions are implicitly the most direct challenge to the relevance of divine power in human affairs, the Court's decisions to legalize abortion on demand is an even more shocking defiance of divinely ordered morality. The assumptions of the Court in its school-prayer opinions and the humanistic view of man as lacking an important spiritual dimension set the stage for its abortion decisions.

The Supreme Court could deny the right to life only by refusing to deal with the biological humanity of the unborn child. So the Court ducked that fundamental question and stated simply that it need not confront the difficult question of when life begins. Of course, *this is the one question* that the Court absolutely had to answer in making its decision. Having dragged out all the cliches, all the misstatements of legal history, the Court proceeded to avoid the bottom line. The Court lacked the courage to confront the inevitable, basic question—the only question that really matters in this controversy: What about the deliberate termination of innocent human life?

Sometime ago I paid a visit to Duke University Medical Center, to visit a friend of mine who is in charge of the Children's Hospital. There must have been fifty beds there, with tiny little human beings in each, born prematurely, being given every conceivable life-supporting treatment with millions of dollars worth of sophisticated equipment and technology. And right across the corridor in the waiting room I saw mothers and fathers on their knees, praying that their babies across the corridor would live; waiting hopefully for an encouraging report from the physicians and the nurses.

It occurred to me: What a contradiction! Here in this hospital is the expenditure of millions of dollars, and dedicated service by highly trained medical personnel working around the clock, to save the lives of those little ones. I returned to Washington that evening, and the very next day I found myself in a pitched battle on the Senate floor, resisting efforts by senators to appropriate millions of dollars of the taxpayers' money to destroy the lives of literally countless thousands of innocent unborn children.

Once the principle of the sanctity of innocent human life is discarded, we are on a slippery slope toward the violation of everybody's human rights. Remember what the Supreme Court stated: Only viable human beings who have the capability for meaningful life may—but need not!—be protected by the state. As Everett Koop and Francis Schaeffer suggest, this statement could be a death warrant for untold numbers of human beings in a few years.

A recent article in the prestigious Stanford Law Review finds a pervasive practice of withholding ordinary medical care, and even food, from handicapped infants, and it concludes that the United States has embarked upon a silent and widespread program of euthanasia.

This is precisely why I believe Congress must act to protect all innocent human life. And that is why I have introduced an amendment to the Constitution to guarantee the right to life during each stage of human development.

The language of my human-life amendment is very simple. Senate Joint Resolution 12 states: "The paramount right to life is vested in each human being from the moment of fertilization without regard to age, health, or condition of dependency." If passed by the Congress and ratified by the legislatures of three-fourths of the states, it would bring to an end the more than 1,374,000 abortions performed in the United States annually. This amendment would also restore our nation's legal recognition of the sanctity of innocent human life whether existing in the womb, the intensive care nursery, a mental hospital, or a nursing home.

The Supreme Court's decisions concerning both school prayer and abortion strike at the very basis of the family's right over the education and upbringing of children. Indeed, legal scholars are beginning to speculate as to whether the family itself is still constitutional.

Throughout history the family has been a remarkably resilient institution. It has survived famines, wars, and plagues. Yet, it remains to be seen whether the family can survive the destructive activity of the federal government. The federal government, which the founding fathers envisioned would support the natural institutions of society such as the family, has instead worked against them. Today the family is threatened by a combination of special interests that sees government as the only legitimate institution in society.

Consider, for example, the 1980 White House Conference on Families. At first the conference was to be called the White House Conference on the Family. But its organizers decided that the term "family" was too narrow. So they discarded the traditional definition of "family" as a relationship by blood, marriage, or adoption and substituted a new definition stating that a family consists of two or more persons related by reasons of mutual support and living under the same roof. The conference leaders contend that this new definition better reflects the "differences in structure and lifestyle" in America, and hence the change of the terms.

With this astonishing mandate, it was not too surprising when the chairman of the conference announced that organizations such as the National Gay Task Force "will be a major resource" for the White House Conference on Families. With such "major resources," I dread to see the new federal policies the White House conference will recommend to the Congress.

Christians understand that the family is not simply some stage in man's anthropological development. The family is ordained by God as the best and first society in which mankind participates. It is the most fulfilling means for the care and nurturing of children and the association of men and women. Even our Lord himself was part of a family and was subject to the discipline of His parents and learned from them. We should consider the family—and not the city or state—as the primary unit in which people live out their lives.

Isn't it time that Christians across America insist that the rights and duties of the family are independent of government? Isn't this especially true concerning the fundamental right of parents in the education of their children? Consider the recent attempt by the Internal Revenue Service to impose admission quotas on private, church-related schools.

The IRS action was not an attempt to protect anyone's civil rights. It was a callous, and in my view, unlawful attempt to take over and control the Christian schools of this nation. It was an attack upon the basic rights of parents to determine the education and religious upbringing of their children.

After two days of debate in the Senate, an amendment I had offered was passed in 1979, prohibiting the IRS from taking further action on its new proposals. That amendment has not become the law. It was attached to legislation of only one year's duration. This year we will be forced to confront the issue again.

We must continue to insist that the rearing of children is the right of the family—not the federal government. There is no such thing as a "value-free" education. The absence of moral principles and religious values is a principle in itself—a very dangerous one.

Christian schools, which are being organized at a rate of three new schools each day, are one of the best hopes for the continued greatness of our nation. We need to take every opportunity in the Congress to preserve their independence.

The Conservative Trend
in Congress

by Senator Roger W. Jepsen

There is unquestionably a conservative trend in Congress today. This is apparent not only from the voting records of congressmen and senators, but in the tone of debate within Congress and the absence of major new liberal initiatives. Liberal proposals that would have breezed through Congress in years past are not even introduced today. Conservative proposals that would never have been considered earlier are now becoming law. More and more often the conservatives are finding themselves joined in their effort by longtime liberals who see the political wind blowing in a different direction (especially when they are up for reelection). I expect that this trend will be strengthened by future elections.

This conservative trend was most evident in the 1978 elections. In June, California voters overwhelmingly approved Proposition 13. In the November elections the trend continued, with many prominent liberals losing to conservatives. In addition to my own victory over Senator Dick Clark (who was by every measure the most liberal member of the U.S. Senate), conservatives defeated liberals in the races listed on the following page.

This is only a partial list, of course. In addition, there were numerous conservative victories in races for the U.S. House of Representatives, state assembly, state senate, and local government. In 1976, 42% of the total votes cast in House of Repre-

Conservative Victories in 1978

Conservative winner	*Liberal loser*	*Race*
Gordon Humphrey	Thomas McIntyre	U.S. Senate (N.H.)
Robert Short	Donald Fraser	Democratic Primary (U.S. Senate, Minn.)
Ed King	Michael Dukakis	Democratic Primary (Governorship, Mass.)
Jeff Bell	Clifford Case	Republican Primary (U.S. Senate, N.J.)
Bill Armstrong	Floyd Haskell	U.S. Senate (Colo.)
Rudy Boschwitz	Wendell Anderson	U.S. Senate (Minn.)
William Cohen	William Hathaway	U.S. Senate (Maine)
Bill Clements	John Hill	Governorship (Texas)
Richard Thornburgh	Pete Flaherty	Governorship (Pa.)
Albert Quie	Rudy Perpich	Governorship (Minn.)
Larry Pressler	Don Barnett	U.S. Senate (S.D.)
Lee Dreyfus	Martin Schreiber	Governorship (Wisc.)
Thad Cochran	Maurice Danton	U.S. Senate (Miss.)

sentatives races went to Republicans, while in 1978 this increased to 45%. In 1976 Democrats received 54.5% of all votes cast in Senate races, but in 1978 they received only 50.5% of such votes.

The conservative trend in the United States should also be seen in the context of a worldwide conservative trend. In 1979 there were spectacular victories by the Conservative Party in Great Britain and Canada. In 1978 the socialists, who had governed Sweden for almost half a century, were replaced by moderates. In 1977 Israel replaced the Labor Party, which had ruled the nation since independence in 1948, with the conservative Likud Party. And in many other nations, including France, Australia, Japan, and Spain, voters have brought to power conservative governments in the 1970's. In virtually no democratic country has there been a move to the left in recent years.

The impact of the 1978 elections in the United States is already apparent in Senate voting patterns. According to Americans for Democratic Action, a liberal group, there was an across the board conservative trend in Senate voting, with the Senate's overall liberal rating dropping from 42 in 1978 to 38 in 1979.

The ADA ratings are confirmed by other ratings as well. *Congressional Quarterly*, for example, reports:

The conservative coalition of Southern Democrats and Republicans gained considerable strength in Congress in 1979. Although the conservative voting alliance showed up in 1979 on about the same proportion of House and Senate recorded votes as it did in 1978, it emerged victorious a significantly larger percentage of the time. The coalition won 70 percent of the votes on which it appeared in 1979, compared to only a 52 percent success rate in 1978.

CQ also notes that "most of the liberal senators up for reelection in 1980 and targeted for defeat by conservative groups showed more support for the coalition in 1979 than they had in 1978. Making the largest jump in this group was Frank Church, D-Idaho, who supported the coalition position 47 percent of the time in 1979, compared to 31 percent in 1978."

Frank Church is not an isolated example. An examination of the voting records of all liberal senators up for reelection in 1980 shows a considerable increase in conservative voting by many of them. The following table shows the increase in conservative voting by some of these senators based on ratings done by the American Conservative Union:

American Conservative Union Senate Ratings

Senator	Cumulative Rating	1979 Rating	% Change
Gary Hart (Colo.)	10	27	+ 170
Mike Gravel (Alaska)	17	38	+ 123
John Durkin (N.H)	16	30	+ 87
George McGovern (S.D.)	6	10	+ 66
Dale Bumpers (Ark.)	19	30	+ 58
Frank Church (Idaho)	16	21	+ 31

In other words, not only did the elections of 1978 send to Congress a more conservative group of senators, but their election pushed those senators up for reelection in a more conservative direction. (It should be noted that liberal senators almost always vote more conservatively when they are up for reelection. They assume that voters' memories are not long enough to remember liberal votes early in their terms, and only in years just prior to reelection do they vote as their constituents would prefer them to; that is, conservatively.)

In nations with parliamentary forms of government it is possible for changes in public opinion to be translated into government policy quickly. In the United States, however, because elected officials serve fixed terms of varying length, it may take some time before a change in public opinion is reflected in policy. Thus, we are only slowly seeing the effect of a conservative trend in public opinion in congressional representation.

Virtually every public opinion poll taken in recent years has documented a move to the right by Americans. In a poll taken by Gallup in August 1978, 43% described their political position as "right of center," whereas 20% classified themselves as "left of center." Earlier in the year a CBS News/*New York Times* poll reported that the ratio of self-described conservatives to liberals was 42 to 23%.

Perhaps more significantly, college students have moved dramatically to the right in the last several years. In 1970, 37% of first-year college students identified their political beliefs as liberal or far left. By 1978, that proportion had dropped to 26%. Thus a report on student political opinion taken during the 1977-78 academic year makes this observation:

> Liberalism has peaked; its high water mark is visible on every question on every campus. Only radicalism is ebbing faster, having declined 40% in eight years, to the point where on the average campus only one student in ten calls himself a radical. Conservatism, by contrast, is everywhere recrudescent, its strength greater than at any time since the early 1960s. Three-fifths of today's undergraduates approve of right-to-work laws, and a majority opposes the socialization of basic industries. A resounding 63% think that affirmative action in the form of preferential college admissions for blacks is unfair. Four out of five believe in God (in some form), and three-quarters consider themselves members of an organized religion. Given the choice of war or surrender in a confrontation with the Soviet Union, 56% would have the United States fight.

There are two important reasons why I expect these conservative trends to continue, not only among students but throughout the country. The first reason is that inflation and rising taxes, resulting from people being pushed up into higher tax brackets, are going to make people very suspicious of liberal spending programs, fuel pressure for a balanced budget, and increase support for a tax revolt. Secondly, incidents such as the holding of American hostages by Iranian militants and the Soviet invasion of Afghanistan are going to cause Americans to take a harder line on foreign policy.

Thus, in a recent Louis Harris survey, 85% of the people felt that "politicians promise tax relief before elections and then do nothing about it when elected." Seventy-five percent believe that "people in power don't know how much taxes cause people like me to suffer."

It is certainly not surprising that people feel this way when we have a tax system that causes people to pay higher taxes with every increase in their nominal income, even if inflation has completely wiped out any real income gain. Unfortunately, President Carter is trying to sell Congress on the idea that rising taxes are a good thing in the fight against inflation. Nothing could be further from the truth. Inflation is caused by too many dollars chasing too few goods. When taxes rise it does not change the number of dollars in circulation, it merely redirects them away from the private sector to government. And insofar as higher taxes discourage work, production and investment, they make inflation worse.

Fortunately, the Congress seems more aware of these facts than the President. The 1978 tax cut, passed by Congress over the president's objections, was the first tax cut in fifteen years directed toward increasing investment rather than pumping up demand. The Congress resoundingly rejected the "tax reform" proposals made by President Carter because it understood that tax reform is just a euphemism for tax increase. Congress then proposed to cut the capital gains tax, which had been increased in 1969, and cut tax rates for corporations and taxpayers across the board.

In another example of a conservative trend in congressional economic policy, the Joint Economic Committee in 1979 issued its first consensus report in more than twenty years. Unanimously approved by all Republicans and Democrats on the committee (including such liberals as Senators Kennedy, Ribicoff, McGovern, and Sarbanes), the report made explicit recommendations for a tighter monetary policy, business tax cuts to improve productivity, and a reduction in government spending. In effect, the Democrats adopted the traditional conservative Republican position.

In foreign policy it is easier to point to specific actions that indicate a conservative trend. In 1979 the Congress reversed a long-standing policy of cutting the defense budget and instead endorsed a substantial increase. It is the general opinion of all senators now that such increases will have to be made for at least the next several years in order to compensate for earlier cuts in both conventional and strategic forces. This shift parallels the views of the American people. According to a recent Gallup Poll twice as many people now feel that defense spending is too low as think it is too high. As recently as 1973 five times as many people thought defense spending was too high as thought it was too low.

The truth is that for years the Congress has been paying for increased welfare and social spending by cutting the defense budget in both real and nominal terms. Throughout most of the 1970s Congress cut the President's requested defense budget while increasing overall spending.

Now the situation almost seems to be reversed, with the President trying to hold down defense spending while Congress increases it over his objections. Unfortunately, even with substantial increases in defense spending it will be many years before we make up for the time lost when important programs, such as the B-1 bomber and the antiballistic missile system, were canceled for lack of funds. The important thing is that we get started on a rearmament program quickly and not waver in our determination.

The conservative trend in Congress is being reinforced by increasing social conservatism. Throughout the country, people are rediscovering traditional values of family, religion, and self-reliance. As a Christian, I find this heartening. People are fed up with permissiveness in public schools, on television, and in social behavior. There is evidence of these facts all around us.

In religion, people are turning away from more liberal churches and embracing more fundamentalist denominations. Thus forty percent of the people interviewed in 1978 said that they had been "born again," or had a "born-again experience"—that is, an identifiable turning point in their life.

In education, people are turning away from public schools and increasingly sending their children to private schools, especially private religious schools. These parents seek schools where they have greater control over what their children are taught and where youths will associate with children who hold Christian views. This new movement has no relationship to an earlier trend toward private schools that maintained segregation. Many parents are also sending their children to private schools because of their belief that educational basics have been ignored by public schools.

Congress has responded to this situation by showing great interest in tuition tax credit proposals, which would give people a tax break for sending their children to private schools.

In law, one can see that people are less than enthusiastic about proposals considered more liberal, such as the Equal Rights Amendment and the enforced "quota system" of affirmative action. They are simultaneously increasing their support for conservative proposals to restrict abortions—especially public funding for abortions—and allow voluntary prayer in school. Every year, for example, The House of Representatives overwhelmingly approves the so-called Hyde Amendment to restrict government funding for abortions. Although some in the Senate fight the Hyde language, in 1979 the Senate was forced to accept it. And in Massachusetts, the state legislature has approved legislation permitting voluntary prayer in school.

In many other social and cultural areas one can observe a return to fundamentals—in music, art, fashion, and theater. The wild, *avant-garde* styles of earlier years seem now to be out of favor.

There is a conservative trend in Congress and politics. It is reinforced by the world military situation, the domestic economic situation, and by social and cultural trends as well. Liberals have been in control of Congress for 44 out of the last 48 years. And we have had more of the same—more government, more taxation, and more regulations.

I think Americans are ready for a change. I do not wish to give the impression that those who hold a more liberal philosophy are not well-intentioned. I know many who are fine, hard working, committed Christian people. However, I do expect that more conservatives will be elected to Congress to turn back the liberal tide, rather than merely fighting a rear guard action against it.

The Law and Liberty

by Carl A. Anderson

Abraham Lincoln's description, in the Gettysburg Address, of the American republic as "a new nation, conceived in liberty" can be credited with more than just historical accuracy. It points to an underlying passion that runs throughout the American political tradition: the passion for liberty. Yet Americans are contentious as to the meaning of the word "liberty." For the founding fathers it meant the right to self-government. For Lincoln it meant freedom from bondage. For the pilgrims at Plymouth it meant freedom to worship God without constraint.

Today, claims in the name of liberty are at the root of many political controversies. Whether the issue is private education, school prayer, abortion, or civil rights, the debate usually involves a claim of freedom. However, the actual content of the freedoms being asserted is often very different. Rather than viewing freedom as the ability to do what is right, freedom is usually considered in only a negative sense, as the absence of restraint.

The early Christians thought that freedom is always linked to a dependence on something else, and that this dependence signifies the content and meaning of freedom. The apostle Paul spoke of this concept of freedom in the epistle to the Romans:

> Know ye not, that to whom ye yield yourselves servants to obey, his servants ye are to whom ye obey; whether of sin unto death, or of

obedience unto righteousness? But God be thanked, that ye were the servants of sin, but ye have obeyed from the heart that form of doctrine which was delivered you. Being then made free from sin, ye became the servants of righteousness. . . . For when ye were the servants of sin, ye were free from righteousness. . . . But now being made free from sin, and become servants to God, ye have your fruit unto holiness, and the end everlasting life (Romans 6:16-22).

Freedom cannot be separated from reality; and for the Christian, a person attains freedom in precisely the degree to which he becomes dependent upon ultimate reality. In the deepest sense, liberty is only possible when man conforms his life to the conditions of his existence and the laws that define them. On the other hand, understood as merely the absence of restraint, freedom becomes a not-so-subtle form of bondage to the unfettered human will and appetite.

"The law of the Spirit of life in Christ Jesus hath made me free from the law of sin and death" (Romans 8:2). Not only is the freedom of the Christian life made possible through this dependence upon the supernatural, but liberty and justice in the natural order are equally dependent on a clear perception of reality. Personal freedom is maximized to the extent that human action is anchored to the natural order, especially as reflected in the natural institutions of society.

Foremost among them is the family. The civil liberties enjoyed in the United States have in large measure been preserved through the continued vitality of strong independent social institutions such as the family. American democracy has recognized that the individual's "dependence" upon the institutions of family, church, and local community provide the best protection against an excessive dependence upon government. During the last decade, the various "liberation movements" that seek the release of individuals from their relationship of rights and duties concerning the family have produced a greater dependence upon government for the delivery of services and the development of values. For example, advocates of "women's liberation" have found that their new freedom from "sexual stereotypes" requires an increased reliance upon government to provide free day care centers, abortions, and job training.

The increasing legal attack upon the family as the fundamental institution of society, marks an assault against personal liberty. Yet, the legal framework for the undermining of the family has in large measure been developed by the Supreme Court in the name of freedom. For example, in the case of *Eisenstadt v. Baird*, the Court stated that "the marital couple is not an independent entity with a mind and heart of its own, but an association of two individuals, each with a separate intellectual and emotional makeup."[1] In the Court's view, marriage is no longer a special union that brings into being that unique entity, the family. Instead, the family is simply an association of individuals bound together by certain legal relationships that a court or legislature may expand or diminish.

The view of human society reflected in so many of the Supreme Court's recent decisions found its inception in the philosophy of Thomas Hobbes. Hobbes held that, prior to the creation of society, man lived a completely individual existence in the "state of nature." In this condition, prehistoric man had a hermit-like existence and was totally free. Inasmuch as there was neither society nor government, there was no law or moral code preventing men from doing whatever they liked. Freedom was limited only by fear. Indeed, Hobbes' description of the state of nature is, to say the least, unpleasant.

> In such condition, there is no place for industry; because the fruit thereof is uncertain: and consequently no culture of the earth; no navigation; nor use of the commodities that may be imported by sea; no commodious building; . . . no account of time; no arts; no letters; no society; and which is worst of all, continual fear, and danger of violent death; and the life of man, solitary, poor, nasty, brutish, and short.[2]

Hobbes theorized that in order to escape such an intolerable situation, men came together and ratified the "social contract." Men, through their mutual consent, formed society and created government to establish law and keep order. Society, government, and law are, in Hobbes' scheme, creations of man that are voluntarily accepted as a matter of convenience. None of these creations have any higher sanction than utility—they are useful in combating the barbarities that result from freedom.

Hobbes' view contradicted the Christian understanding of society. Christian jurists had based the bridge between moral man and society in the classical philosophy of natural law. Beginning with Plato, the natural law tradition holds that man has always been a social being; dependent on others, he has always lived within a social setting. Human society is more than a mere herd gathered together for self-preservation and mutual enrichment. Man is different from all other animals in that he possesses the ability to speak and, therefore, is able to contemplate and discuss the nature of right and wrong, justice and injustice. By his very nature, man seeks to know and live by justice; and human society demands justice.

The classical philosophers saw that the laws that govern the way man should act are discovered within man himself. The need for society, government, and law, and the desire and the pursuit of justice, are not things that man creates or that he chooses to make his life more convenient and comfortable. Rather, these needs are inherent within man. They are laws by which he must live if he is to be truly human.

The natural law speculation of the ancient philosophers was readily accepted by the early Christians who relied on Paul. "For when the Gentiles, which have not the law, do by nature the things contained in the law, these, having not the law, are a law unto themselves" (Romans 2:14). During the Middle Ages the concept was more fully developed by such thinkers as Thomas Aquinas. As Etienne Gilson explained:

> All beings created by God and maintained in existence by His will, can be regarded as one huge society in which all of us are members, along with animals, and even with things. There is not a single creature, animate or inanimate, which does not act in conformity with certain ends. Animals and things are subject to these rules and tend toward their ends without knowing them. Man, on the contrary, is conscious of them, and his moral justice consists in accepting them voluntarily.[3]

Unlike earlier pagan philosophers, Christian thinkers were able to come to a greater understanding of why man must live according to certain moral precepts if he is to become truly human and truly free. Man, like all of nature, is the creation of the Almighty, who made man according to His own image. The moral law imprinted in man's nature is essential to his quest for perfection.

Natural law became the foundation for English common law. Sir Edward Coke, the noted seventeenth-century English jurist, described the "law of nature" as "that which God at the time of creation of the nature of man infused into his heart, for his preservation and direction. . . . The law of nature is written with the finger of God in the heart of man."[4]

This understanding of natural law was brought to colonial America and influenced the development of early American law through the *Commentaries on the Law of England* by William Blackstone. With the exception of the Bible, the *Commentaries* was the most widely read book in early America. Blackstone maintained that God was the author of all true law whether found in revelation or by unaided reason. According to Blackstone, "Upon these two foundations, the law of nature and the law of revelation, depend all human laws. That is to say, no human laws should be suffered to contradict these."[5]

Natural law theory found a prominent place in the early constitutional law of the United States. Justice Joseph Story, an advocate of natural law and an early member of the Supreme Court, relied on natural law in writing many of the Court's opinions. He defined natural law in the following way:

> Natural Law, or, as it is commonly called, the law of nature, is that system of principles, which human reason has discovered to regulate the conduct of man in all his various relations. In its largest sense . . . it comprehends man's duties to God, to himself, to other men, and as a member of political society.
>
> The obligatory force of the law of nature upon man is derived from its presumed coincidence with the will of his Creator. God has fashioned man according to his own good pleasure, and has fixed the laws of his being, and determined his powers and faculties. He has the supreme right to prescribe the rules, to which man shall regulate his conduct, and the means, by which he shall obtain happiness and avoid misery. . . . The whole duty of man therefore consists in two things; first, in making constant efforts to ascertain what is the will of God; and, secondly, in obedience to that will when ascertained.[6]

The development of natural law theory rests on the premise that there are identifiable, unchanging "natures" inherent in the existing things that populate the world. In knowing an object, such as a particular man or a tree, the human intellect is able to consider the object's essence or nature in the form of a concept. This understanding of man's intellectual ability has a Biblical foundation in the second chapter of Genesis when Adam is commanded to name the animals. In the Hebrew, the phrase "to name" signifies more than just a casual designation; it includes an understanding of the object and an actual definition of it.

Opposed to this philosophy are the theories of nominalism and relativism, which maintain that such concepts and universals are not derived from the true nature of real existing things, but are only words or names used as a matter of convenience.

This philosophical dispute has profound implications for the development of law. Since a nominalist or relativist has lost the ability to say that there is an identifiable human nature and that this nature can be recognized in each existing man, he has lost the ability to determine that a man is more important than some other existing thing.

Supreme Court Justice Oliver Wendell Holmes, perhaps the most influential jurist in our century, well represented this mentality in American law. Holmes wrote, "I see no reason for attributing to man a significance different in kind from that which belongs to a baboon or to a grain of sand."[7] Not only is the value of a human life undermined by the inability to deal with the nature of an object, but it also becomes impossible to perceive truth by the aid of reason. For Holmes, the truth is not something corresponding to reality but is merely "the majority vote of the nation that could lick all others."[8] Holmes' relativistic view of man and of truth reduced law from a pursuit of reason to a struggle for power. When considering the nature of law, Holmes believed, "the ultimate question is what do the dominant forces of the community want and do they want it hard enough to disregard whatever inhibitions may stand in their way."[9]

This philosophy of relativism has been echoed by many members of the Supreme Court since Holmes. For example, in 1951, Chief Justice Fred Vinson wrote:

> Nothing is more certain in modern society than the principle that there are no absolutes, that a name, a phrase, a standard has meaning only when associated with the considerations which give birth to nomenclature . . . all concepts are relative.[10]

Applied to our laws, the philosophy of relativism could be counted on to produce the Supreme Court's 1973 abortion decision in *Roe v. Wade*. There, the basis of the Court's action was its inability to understand the nature of man and to ascribe any value to it. The Court brushed away the central issue in the case—the termination of innocent human life—with the casual explanation that "we need not resolve the difficult question of when life begins."[11] One suspects the Justices' refusal to confront the question of what constitutes a human being in large measure arises from the Court's hesitation to answer the logically prior question as to what constitutes human nature.

The wall of separation between reason and reality produced by nominalism and relativism severs the law from reality when those philosophies are adopted by jurists. For example, when New York passed legislation in 1970 permitting abortion on demand during the first six months of pregnancy, a suit was brought on the basis that the law was an unconstitutional infringement of the right to life. The case rested on the extensive medical evidence and other documentation that the unborn child was indeed a human being. Although the highest court of New York ruled that the unborn child was "human" and "unquestionably alive," it nonetheless rejected a claim to a right to life on the basis that "it is not true that the legal order corresponds to the natural order."[12]

This triumph of the judicial will is an extraordinary expression of the lengths permitted judges in establishing the judiciary as an independent institution. Yet, it is precisely this "freedom" of the lawmaker from the higher authority of the natural law and moral order that prepares the way for the absolute loss of freedom and justice. It was no coincidence that the sudden loss of freedom in Germany during the 1930's followed several decades of effort to liberate the German judiciary from any claims of a moral order superior to itself.

It is doubtful whether meaningful personal liberty can continue to exist even in the United States if such a complete separation between law and reality continues. The Christian must continue to insist that liberty is only possible when a society's legal system conforms to reality, for justice is only possible when law relates to the natural order of things. The Christian view, as articulated by Augustine, finds that dependence on God and on His law is the indispensable condition for human liberty, not only for each individual on a personal level, but for society at large. Charles Norris Cochrane observed that, while Augustine fully understood the limitations of political action, he nonetheless believed that:

> Ultimately, there can be no compromise between the claims of Caesar and those of Christ. Caesar must therefore abandon his pretension to independence and submit to Christian principles, or he must be prepared for the doom which awaits sin and error in its secular conflict with justice and truth. . . . Accordingly, to admit as final any dualism

between "moral man" and "immoral society" is to perpetrate the most vicious of heresies; it is to deny the Christian promise and to subvert the foundation of the Christian hope.[13]

The fact that man must live out his life in the community of others places a duty upon the Christian to work to transform the society in which he lives into one where sufficient liberty exists so that the job of evangelism is possible. Ultimately, the Christian must strive for a society in which the precepts of natural justice are followed and it is possible to live the Christian life without heroic sacrifice. Historically, Christianity has always maintained such a strong public character with Christians seeking to affect the political and legal institutions of their society. Yet, in the United States, the influence of Christianity in the public life of the nation has gradually diminished. Harvard law professor Harold Berman has observed:

> . . . in the nineteenth century and even more so in the twentieth [there] has been the very gradual reduction of the traditional religions to the level of a personal, private matter, without public influence on legal development, while other belief systems—new secular religions ("ideologies," "isms")—have been raised to the level of passionate faiths.[14]

Perhaps the most pervasive of these "new secular religions" is secular humanism, which has been defined as follows:

> The word "secular" by definition refers to the temporal rather than the spiritual. "Secularism" is a doctrinal belief that morality is based solely in regard to the temporal well-being of mankind to the exclusion of all belief in God, a supreme being, or a future eternity. "Humanism" is a philosophy or attitude that is concerned with human beings, their achievement and interests, and the condition or quality of being human, rather than with the abstract beings and problems of theology.[15]

Yet, secular humanism is by nature religious, in that it takes the place of theism in the lives of its adherents. The manifestos of secular humanism, *Humanist Manifesto I* (1933) and *Humanist Manifesto II* (1973), both set forth what appear to be doctrinal statements of a newly articulated religion. Indeed, *Humanist Manifesto I* begins by stating, "In order that religious humanism may better be understood, we, the undersigned, desire to make certain affirmations. . . ." It continues, "Any religion that can hope to be a synthesizing and dynamic force today must be shaped for the needs of this age. To establish such a religion is a major necessity of the present."[16]

In this sense, the secular humanism of the twentieth century is surprisingly similar to the philosophy of the eighteenth century Enlightenment, which marked the first substantial effort in Western civilization to separate society's moral order from Christian truths. Like our own age, the Enlightenment has been considered an age of science and reason as opposed to one of faith. As Carl Becker has pointed out, the advocates of the Enlightenment were at the same time too skeptical and too credulous. "They denied that miracles ever happened, but believed in the perfectibility of the human race."[17]

The new religion of secular humanism is rapidly replacing Christianity as the public orthodoxy of the United States. Already, the free exercise of religion, guaranteed by the First Amendment, is coming to mean simply that the Christian life may be lived in private, but not in public. The decisions of the Supreme Court prohibiting voluntary prayer in public schools reflect this rejection of any public acknowledgement of God.

The concern over the increasing secularization of America reflects the fact that no society can remain neutral concerning the basic moral questions confronting its members. The resolution of these questions must affect the law, since laws are the embodiment of society's moral consensus. More than forty years ago, T. S. Eliot, with remarkable foresight, warned that to consider ourselves a Christian society "is an abuse of terms. We mean only that we have a society in which no one is penalised for the *formal profession* of Christianity."[18] As the non-Christian elements of society become more pronounced, Christians are becoming entangled in a network of social institutions that have ceased to be neutral and are now positively anti-Christian. As *Christianity Today* editorialized in 1973:

> . . . Christians should accustom themselves to the thought that the American state no longer supports, in any meaningful sense, the laws of God, and prepare themselves spiritually for the prospect that it may one day formally repudiate them and turn against those who seek to live by them.[19]

This is not to say that a Christian must therefore seek to impose articles of the Christian faith through the sanction of the law. The supernatural obligations proper to the life of grace within the Christian faith are not to be confused with those requirements of natural justice that reason commands all persons to respect.

It is, however, precisely because of the Christian's relationship with and understanding of the Author of the natural law that he is able to uniquely defend the precepts of natural justice for all members of society. And it is in just this sense that government may properly encourage the free exercise of religion and remove many social barriers to living the Christian life. The authors of the Constitution and the Bill of Rights sought to shape a system of government that would encourage the preservation of our nation's religious heritage. The demands by advocates of the Enlightenment and the French Revolution that religion and its moral authority be divorced from the operation of the law were repeatedly and explicitly rejected by the architects of the American system.

George Washington, for example, in his farewell address, clearly rejected the notion that the dictates of religion should be separated from the public life of the nation. Washington observed:

> Of all the dispositions and habits which lead to political prosperity, religion and morality are indispensable supports. In vain would that man claim the tribute of patriotism, who should labor to subvert these great pillars of human happiness. The mere politician, equally with the pious man, ought to respect and to cherish them. . . . Reason and experience both forbid us to expect that national morality can prevail in exclusion of religious principle.[20]

If the founding fathers were correct when they concluded that freedom and justice were possible, within the American republic or elsewhere, only when founded upon the moral authority of Christianity, then today's Christian citizen faces no greater task than to protect and enlarge the freedom of the church. For by enabling the church to pursue its historic mission of evangelization and of reform according to the authority of the Gospel, the Christian preserves and strengthens as well the intellectual and legal foundations of freedom.

---

[1]Eisenstadt v. Baird, 405 U.S. 438, 453 (1972).

[2]Thomas Hobbes, *Leviathan,* ed. M. Oakeshott (New York: Macmillan, 1977), p. 100.

[3]Etienne Gilson, *The Christian Philosophy of St. Thomas Aquinas* (New York: Arno Press, 1956), p. 266

[4]Calvin's Case, 7 Coke's Rep., 1 (a), 77 Eng. Rep. 377, 392 (1610).

[5]William Blackstone, *Commentaries on the Law of England* (1866), p. 28.

[6]Joseph Story, "Natural Law" (1836): reprinted in James McClellan, *Joseph Story and the American Constitution* (Norman, Oklahoma: University of Oklahoma Press, 1971), p. 313.

[7]*The Pollack—Holmes Letters: Correspondence of Sir Frederick Pollack and Mr. Justice Holmes 1874-1932*, Vol. 2 (Cambridge, Massachusetts: Harvard University Press, 1942), p. 252.

[8]Oliver W. Holmes, *The Natural Law: Collected Legal Papers* (1920), p. 310.

[9]Francis A. Schaeffer, *How Should We Then Live?* (Old Tappan, New Jersey: Revell, 1976), p. 217.

[10]*Barrons,* June 18, 1951.

[11]Roe v. Wade, 410 U.S. 113, 157 (1973); see also Francis A. Schaeffer and C. Everett Koop, *Whatever Happened to the Human Race?* (Revell, 1979) and Charles E. Rice, *Beyond Abortion: The Theory and Practice of the Secular State* (Franciscan Herald, 1979).

[12]Byrn v. New York City Health and Hospitals Corp., 31 N.Y. 2d 194, 286 N.E. 2d 887, 889 (1972); appeal dismissed, 410 U.S. 940 (1973).

[13]Charles Norris Cochrane, *Christianity and Classical Culture* (Oxford, England: Oxford University Press, 1944), p. 510.

[14]Harold Berman, *The Interaction of Law and Religion* (1974), p. 68.

[15]John Whitehead and John Conlan, "The Establishment of the Religion of Secular Humanism and Its First Amendment Implications," *Texas Tech Law Review,* 1978, pp. 29, 30.

[16]Paul Kurtz (intro. by), *Humanist Manifesto I and II* (Buffalo, New York: Prometheus Books, 1973).

[17]Carl Becker, *The Heavenly City of the Eighteenth-Century Philosophers* (New Haven, Connecticut: Yale University Press, 1932), p. 31.

[18]T. S. Eliot, *The Idea of a Christian Society* (1940), p. 5.

[19]*Christianity Today,* February 16, 1973, p. 32.

[20]Henry Commager, ed., *Documents of American History* (New York: Appleton, 1968), p. 169.